From Liquor to Dhikr

Islam and the 12 Steps

James H.

PathWays Collective, LLC

This book is dedicated to all those struggling with the disease of addiction. May you find hope in these pages and discover that there is, indeed, a solution.

"There is a principle which is a bar against all information, which is proof against all arguments, and which cannot fail to keep a man in everlasting ignorance—that principle is contempt prior to investigation."

Herbert Spencer, quoted in Alcoholics Anonymous, 4th ed., p. 568

"Do not assume something is false just because you do not understand it. Everything has an explanation, even if it is beyond your comprehension."

Imam Abu Hamid al-Ghazali, Ihya' 'Ulum al-Din

Contents

Acknowledgements

First and foremost, I thank Allah Almighty. By His grace, I have been transformed from a hopeless alcoholic and drug addict into someone with an unburdened heart, striving to walk the path with sincerity. All praise belongs to Him.

I thank the Prophet Muhammad, peace be upon him, whose life and teachings are a lighthouse for the lost. Without his guidance, I would still be adrift.

To my wife, Angela: you have the purest and most loving heart I have ever known. Your compassion and companionship have enriched my life beyond measure. To my children, who continue to inspire me to be a better man—you are my motivation and my legacy.

To my father, who taught me to meet the challenges of life with humor, and to my mother—herself a sober woman—who taught me that when faced with a dilemma, the most loving option is always the right one.

To my brother, Adam, whose wit and intelligence continue to motivate me to grow and think deeper.

To my first sponsor, Mark G., who introduced me to the mystic heart of recovery and helped me recognize the spiritual current running through the Steps. To my current sponsor, Mike K., whose steady guidance and wise counsel help me navigate life on life's terms.

To my Muslim brother, Yahya C., who suggested the title of this book and continues to be a brilliant source of Islamic guidance.

To Ihsan Alexander and the Awakenings Academy—your instruction has deepened my *deen* and, by extension, my sobriety.

To Pero Novak, whose lesson about "recognizing the need where the need isn't there" became the seed that ultimately inspired this book.

And to all the members of Absolute Surrender, my morning sobriety tune-up—you are part of my daily realignment. Thank you for showing up, day after day, with honesty, intention, and fellowship.

Author's Note

This book is an independent work and is not affiliated with or endorsed by Alcoholics Anonymous World Services, Inc. It has also not been reviewed or approved by any Islamic organization, institution, or scholarly authority. The contents reflect the personal experience, strength, and hope of the author as a recovering alcoholic and Muslim revert.

The material presented here does not speak on behalf of AA, nor does it represent a definitive view of Islamic theology, law, or practice. Every effort has been made to respect the Twelve Traditions of Alcoholics Anonymous, particularly those concerning anonymity, affiliation, and non-promotion. Similarly, care has been taken to align with the spiritual and ethical foundations of Islam, while recognizing that interpretations vary across schools and scholars.

This book is not a substitute for professional treatment, a sponsor, or qualified religious guidance. Readers are encouraged to consult addiction professionals, sponsors, and Islamic scholars when navigating personal questions about recovery or practice.

It is offered in the spirit of service, with the sincere intention of supporting those walking the path from addiction to awakening, from disconnection to remembrance, from liquor to *dhikr*.

To Non Muslim Readers

Welcome to From *Liquor to Dhikr: Islam and the 12 Steps*. This book bridges the Twelve Steps of Alcoholics Anonymous (AA) with Islamic spirituality, offering a path to recovery for anyone seeking healing from addiction or spiritual disconnection. You do not need to be Muslim to benefit. Its principles of surrender, hope, and service are universal, resonating with anyone striving to live authentically.

You will encounter Islamic terms such as Qur'an (scripture), *dhikr* (remembrance of God), and *nafs* (ego), which are central to the book's framework. These terms are briefly introduced in a key terms summary and fully defined in the glossary. The abbreviation (SAW) following "Prophet Muhammad" stands for *Ṣallā Allāhu ʿalayhi wa sallam*, which means "peace and blessings be upon him." It is a traditional Muslim expression of reverence used after mentioning the Prophet's name. All Qur'anic translations use the Saheeh International edition for clarity and accessibility.

The tone is raw at times, reflecting the gritty reality of addiction and the culture of recovery in AA. Some of the language may be coarse, though profanity has been avoided. This choice is meant to convey the unfiltered truth of the journey, while always aiming to inspire honesty and hope.

Whether you are in recovery, exploring spirituality, or supporting a loved one, this book invites you to view addiction as a disease that calls for healing and recovery as a spiritual awakening available to all. Take what resonates, leave what does not, and may your journey lead to peace.

To Muslim Readers

A s-salamu alaikum. *From Liquor to Dhikr: Islam and the 12 Steps* brings together the Twelve Steps of Alcoholics Anonymous and Islamic spirituality to support those facing addiction or spiritual disconnection. I am not a scholar. I am an American revert sharing lived experiences as a recovering alcoholic, guided by the Qur'an, Hadith, and the wisdom of Islamic spirituality.

My aim is unity. I recognize Muslims understand addiction in different ways. Some view it through a moral lens; Others as a disease. I understand it as a test from Allah, a call to surrender, and a call to heal.

This book draws from the inward-facing tradition of Islamic spirituality, often known as Sufism, and emphasizes *dhikr* (remembrance), *suhba* (companionship), and *taqwa* (God-consciousness). These concepts align closely with the Twelve Steps and frame recovery as a return to *fitrah* (natural disposition). All hadith referenced are prioritized as *sahih* (authentic), and sources are listed for transparency.

For topics that may raise questions, such as disclosing personal wrongs in Step Five or engaging with the Lord's Prayer in AA meetings, I share examples from my own practice, like using "Ya Allah," and encourage readers to consult scholars for deeper guidance.

Addiction does not reflect weak *iman*. It is a call to submit more deeply to Allah's mercy. Whether you are walking your own path of recovery or supporting someone else, this book offers tools to polish the heart and strengthen your connection to the Divine.

The glossary includes definitions for recovery terms like "the rooms" or "dry drunk," as well as key Islamic terms used throughout the book.

Unless otherwise noted, all Qur'anic translations are from Saheeh International. I chose this translation for its clarity and accessibility. It stays close to the original meaning while using modern English, making it suitable for both Muslim and non-Muslim readers seeking a clear understanding of the Qur'an's message.

Introduction

T his book has been growing inside me for years. It waited quietly and persistently before I ever wrote down an outline. But once I started, the words came quickly. Urgent. Alive. This wasn't a project I chose; it was a purpose I received. I was led here through prayer, and Allah answered.

Resources for Muslims in recovery are scarce. Since I couldn't find the exact book I was looking for, I decided to write it. This is my contribution to a conversation that needs more voices. For some, it may be the book they've been needing but haven't yet found.

I'm not a scholar. I have no formal Islamic credentials, no *ijazah*, and no letters behind my name. I'm not an expert in psychology or a licensed counselor. What I do have is a lifetime of struggling with addiction, finding sobriety, lived experience, and a heart that seeks truth. A heart that has been broken and rebuilt through recovery and Islam. I don't speak from authority. I speak from experience.

Throughout this work, I've leaned heavily on those who do carry authority: the Qur'an, the Hadith of the Prophet Muhammad (SAW), and the writings of scholars and spiritual teachers far beyond my station. You'll see their words throughout these pages—because this book isn't about me. It's about a path. A path that, by the mercy of Allah, I was directed to walk.

I have done my utmost to remain faithful to both the Twelve Steps of Alcoholics Anonymous and the teachings of Islam. I am not a scholar—I'm an American revert, still a novice in my study of Arabic. While I've included some Arabic terms using transliteration throughout the text, I've aimed to make them accessible to readers at all levels. Every Qur'anic verse, hadith, and scholarly quote included in this work has been cited to the best of my ability. I have prioritized authenticated narrations. A list of sources appears at the end of the book for those interested in further exploration. While not exhaustive; some research was drawn from online sources—I have taken care to include only authentic narrations, especially when citing *hadith*, prioritizing those graded as sound (*ṣaḥīḥ*) or strong. My intention throughout has been to preserve the spirit and sincerity of the message, rather than to present a juristic or scholarly treatise.

Recovery and Religion—Two Roads, One Destination

This book exists at the intersection of two spiritual traditions: the Twelve Steps of Alcoholics Anonymous and the path of Islamic spirituality. At first glance, they may seem worlds apart. But anyone familiar with both traditions knows that the gap between them is not as wide as it seems.

What I'm doing here is simple. I'm sharing wisdom I've gained through recovery with Muslims who might need it, and I'm sharing insights from Islam with people in recovery who might benefit. That's it. I'm not rewriting the Big Book. I'm simply passing on the experience, strength, and hope I've received from both paths.

I never took recovery seriously until I found Islam. And I never took Islam seriously until I was in recovery. This book explores the spiritual symbiosis between the two paths, how I've applied both to my life, and what they continue to teach me. If it worked for me, maybe it will work for you too.

I was in recovery long before I reverted to Islam.

And I was learning how to submit to the Will of God long before I took my *shahada*.

The Twelve Steps taught me how to put my ego aside. How to stop performing. How to pray from the heart, not just with my lips. I learned true repentance means making amends, beyond an apology, but making things right. I learned to trust a Power greater than myself. I learned discipline. I learned accountability. Without realizing it, I was being prepared for Islam.

Islam gave me structure where I only had form. It polished the spiritual instincts I had already developed. Where recovery taught me to pray in the morning and before bed, Islam gave me five prayers to weave through the entire day. I learned about fasting, gratitude, submission, and the life of the Prophet (SAW) as the example of excellence in action. I discovered *qadr*, *tawakkul*, *sabr*, and *iman*—concepts I had already tasted in recovery, but now had language for.

Glimpses of God, Then and Now

Through AA, I had glimpses of a spiritual awakening. Moments of clarity. Fleeting serenity. But they were just that—glimpses. Like a fish leaping out of the water, I could see the surface for a moment, then plunge right back into the deep.

Islam gave me a periscope.

Now I can look above the surface whenever I need to. I can orient myself to the Divine at any time. A single "*Bismillah*" reorients my heart. I no longer expect the fleeting moment. I have access. I have tools. I have presence.

AA pointed me to the door.

Islam opened it.

Who This Book Is (and Isn't) For

This book is for anyone battling addiction or spiritual disconnection, offering a path to open your heart through the Twelve Steps and Islam.

If you've ever felt overwhelmed by the pull of this world. Overwhelmed by the noise, the temptations, and the endless hunger of the lower self, then this book is for you. Whether that struggle takes the form of drugs or alcohol, or other compulsions like gambling, sex, food, shopping, or even the quieter sins of the heart like envy or pride, the root is the same: the *nafs*. The ego. The part of us that always wants more and is never satisfied.

My story centers on alcoholism, and my recovery has been shaped by the Twelve Steps of Alcoholics Anonymous. But the deeper work has always been spiritual. What the Steps revealed, and what Islam affirms, is that the real enemy isn't the substance. It's ourselves. The lower part of the self that hungers for escape, control, or numbness at any cost.

Addiction is a disease. A dangerous one. Dangerous in that there is no foreign pathogen that can be medicated away. Dangerous, as in the symptoms are often insidious and take years to manifest fully. Dangerous because of social stigma. Addiction is the only disease that people will yell at you for having. Yet, we must remember to be kind to ourselves if we have this. Having the disease of addiction is not a sign of weak *imam*, rather it is a test, a trial, and an opportunity from Allah to draw closer to Him. Whether you're walking this path as a Muslim or not, this book is for you. It doesn't even matter if you're Muslim, exploring Islam, or simply seeking a spiritual path to recovery, this book offers tools to mend the heart.

Will it please everyone? No.

Muslims are no strangers to debate. We'll split hairs, and then debate how far apart the split hairs need to be before they truly count as split. Some will say this book leans too heavily on AA. Others will say it isn't scholarly enough. Still others will argue it drifts too far into mysticism. That's fine. Critique is part of our tradition. This work was never meant to satisfy every mind. It offers a bridge. A meeting point between recovery and religion, between lived experience and sacred tradition. Controversy is the opposite of my intention. I am aiming for connection and unity.

Recovering addicts aren't exactly known for consensus, either. Anyone who's ever sat through a home group business meeting knows that cooperation is more of an ideal than a reality. Getting sober people to agree on anything is like herding cats. Sharp-clawed, loud, and opinionated cats, who all think they should chair the meeting. Add to that the overt Christian culture that permeates many Western 12-step fellowships, and it's no surprise that some might question whether an Islamic approach to recovery even fits. But recovery, like faith, is not one-size-fits-all. What matters is not the cultural packaging—but the spiritual transformation it produces.

This isn't about winning arguments.

This book is not a theological treatise. It's not a memoir, either. I won't be detailing my personal spiritual journey to Islam, nor will I detail my recovery or my struggles with addiction. I am not here to write out a "drunkalog." If you're wondering, yes, I earned my seat in AA. I've been through the hellish slavery of this disease. From waking up in a stranger's backyard covered in my piss and puke to homelessness, jail, destroyed relationships, suffering multiple relapses, and ruining more than words can capture. This disease is nasty, gritty, dirty, and will take everything from you. It will empty your heart of love and leave only darkness. Yet, from that darkness, led by the grace of Allah, I've also experienced healing. Renewal. Awakening. Truth.

My sponsor Mike K. first asked me, "*What are you willing to do?*"

There was only one answer: **Anything**.

Steps to Sobriety

The Steps are both progressive and cyclical. They're a constant practice. There's no finish line. No one ever fully recovers from this disease. That's why I call myself "recovering." It's a present-tense verb: an ongoing process of healing and spiritual evolution. The Steps are a kind of spiritual alchemy. Turning lead into gold. Shifting from being self-centered to being God-centered.

This mirrors the Islamic path of spiritual growth, where each prayer, each fast, and every act of charity deepens your connection to Allah. What begins as an obligation becomes devotion.

That's the point.

The Big Book says we grow along spiritual lines. Islam says the same.

> *"Indeed, Allah does not change the condition of a people until they change what is in themselves."* (Qur'an 13:11)

That Light, that guidance from Allah, is very real. It's the reality behind our new lease on life.

So, if you see verses repeated or hadith mentioned more than once, know that it's not filler. These truths operate on many levels. What a verse means in Step Two isn't what it means in Step Nine. And after an awakening in Step Twelve, it reveals something else entirely.

The Qur'an doesn't change, but we do. The Steps don't change, but we grow into them.

Why the Sufi Influence?

I'm not a formal Sufi. I don't follow a *sheikh* or belong to a *tariqa*. I have an AA sponsor and work an AA program. I'm deeply influenced by the writings and teachings of the Sufi masters. Why? Because they speak from the heart. And they speak to mine. Their emphasis on presence, surrender, *dhikr* (remembrance), and Divine love resonates deeply with my experience in recovery. The Sufis understood that religion is far more than external compliance; It's about internal transformation. So did the founders of AA.

This book is filled with their wisdom. A reflection of what has helped me. I'm not here to issue rulings. I'm here to attest to what works.

What You'll Find Here

Each chapter in this book is built around one of the Twelve Steps, supported by verses from the Qur'an, insights from Islamic scholars and spiritual teachers, and a consistent focus on internal transformation rather than external performance.

This book is more than just about getting sober. It's about becoming whole.

Crafting a life we won't want to escape. About mending the heart. About awakening to who Allah always intended us to be.

And make no mistake, if untreated, this disease of addiction will kill you. The road ends in jails, institutions, or death. When I go, I'd rather die with the *shahada* on my lips than a bottle in my hand.

If AA taught me anything, it's that transformation is possible. That broken people can be remade. That the worst day of your life can become the foundation for a miracle. And if Islam has taught me anything, it's that all of that happens by the Mercy of Allah alone.

> "No disaster strikes except by permission of Allah. And whoever believes
> in Allah—He will guide his heart. And Allah is Knowing of all things."
> (Qur'an, 64:11)

This work serves as a guide, a companion, and a reflection. It bridges two paths that, when walked with sincerity, are each capable of cultivating spiritual excellence.

This book is not a final word on recovery or Islam, but an invitation to a shared journey. Take what resonates, leave what does not, and may Allah guide us all along the road of happy destiny.

Let's begin.

Essential Islamic Terms

This page introduces key Islamic terms used in From Liquor to Dhikr, with full definitions provided in the appendix glossary. These terms frame addiction as a spiritual test and recovery as a return to Allah's mercy. For non-Muslim readers unfamiliar with Islamic concepts, this list offers guidance to help you navigate the language and deepen your understanding of the spiritual framework woven throughout this work.

- Allah: The Arabic name for God, the singular Creator and Sustainer.

- *Deen*: A complete way of life in submission to Allah that includes belief, worship, and daily conduct.

- *Dhikr*: Remembrance of Allah through phrases like *SubhanAllah* (Glory be to Allah), centering the heart on God.

- *Fitrah*: The innate, pure disposition toward truth and Allah, obscured by addiction but restored through surrender.

- Hadith: Authentic sayings or actions of the Prophet Muhammad (SAW) guiding spiritual and ethical life.

- *Iman*: Inner faith in Allah, strengthened by trust and obedience, vital for recovery.

- *Nafs*: The ego or self, especially *nafs al-ammāra* (commanding self), driving addictive behaviors.

- Qur'an: Islam's holy scripture, a source of guidance and healing.

- *Suhba*: Spiritual companionship, like AA fellowship, supporting sobriety.

- *Taqwa*: God-consciousness, a shield against relapse through awareness of Allah.

- *Tawakkul*: Active trust in Allah's plan, fostering hope in recovery.

For terms like *shari'ah* or *wudu*, see the full glossary. The abbreviation (SAW) stands for, *ṣallā Allāhu ʿalayhi wa sallam*, meaning "peace and blessings be upon him," and is used to honor the Prophet Muhammad.

Essential Recovery Terms

This page introduces key recovery terms from Alcoholics Anonymous (AA), with full definitions in the appendix glossary. For Muslim readers unfamiliar with Recovery concepts, this list offers guidance to help you navigate the language and deepen your understanding of the spiritual framework woven throughout this work. These terms connect AA's Twelve Steps to Islamic spirituality for healing addiction.

1. Big Book: AA's foundational text, *Alcoholics Anonymous*, guiding the Twelve Steps.

2. Ego: The false self, akin to the Islamic *nafs*, fueling addiction.

3. Fellowship: The communal support of AA, like Islamic *suhba*, sustains sobriety.

4. Higher Power: Commonly defined in recovery as "God as we understand Him," this term refers to a power greater than oneself. In this book, it is understood as Allah, the One God in Islamic belief.

5. Insanity: The self-destructive delusion of repeating addictive patterns while expecting a different outcome, confronted directly in Step Two.

6. Powerlessness: Admitting loss of control over addiction, the core of Step One.

7. Resentment: Lingering anger blocking spiritual growth, a relapse trigger.

8. Service: Helping others in recovery, aligning with Islamic *khidmah* (sacred service).

9. Spiritual Awakening: A shift from self to Allah; the goal of the Steps.

10. Sponsor: A sober mentor guiding the Steps, a modern spiritual guide.

For terms like dry drunk or rigorous honesty, see the full glossary. These terms reflect AA's path to transformation.

Chapter One

Surrender to Win

Here marks the beginning of recovery. This chapter explores what it really means to surrender: recognizing it not as defeat, but as the first act of healing. We'll look at how powerlessness, far from being a weakness, can open the door to Divine help. In the Islamic tradition, this mirrors the spiritual discipline of confronting the nafs, the lower self that resists truth and clings to control.

This chapter also lays the foundation for the journey ahead. Clarifying the difference between willpower and willingness, exposing the illusion of control, and introducing the idea that actual strength begins where ego ends. Whether you're new to recovery, new to Islam, or returning to both with a deeper hunger, this is where the path begins: with honesty, humility, and a heart cracked open enough to change.

Step One: We admitted we were powerless over alcohol, that our lives had become unmanageable.

Alcoholics Anonymous (4th Edition):

- "The idea that somehow, someday he will control and enjoy his drinking is the great obsession of every abnormal drinker." — p. 30

- "We learned that we had to fully concede to our innermost selves that we were alcoholics. This is the first step in recovery." — p. 30

Twelve Steps and Twelve Traditions:

- "Who cares to admit complete defeat? Practically no one, of course. Every natural instinct cries out against the idea of personal powerlessness." — p. 21

- "We perceive that only through utter defeat are we able to take our first steps toward liberation and strength." — p. 22

Qur'anic References:

"Indeed, the soul is a persistent enjoiner of evil—except those upon whom my Lord has mercy." (Qur'an, 12:53)

   "Have they not traveled through the land so that they may have hearts by which to reason?" (Qur'an, 22:46)

There's a story in recovery that's been passed around for years. We don't know where it came from, but we all know it's true.

Addiction is like digging a hole.

Every sip of the bottle, every hit of the pipe, every selfish decision—every one of them is another scoop of dirt tossed out of the pit. And before long, you've dug down deep. Far deeper than you meant to go. Too deep to climb out.

The surrounding people — your family, your friends—they see the hole. They see you digging. They know exactly where you're headed. Some try to stop you. Some plead with you to put the shovel down. Some walk away, exhausted and heartbroken. A few lower ropes. Maybe even a ladder. And maybe once or twice, you climb out.

But soon enough, you jump right back in. You may not even know why.

You just can't stop digging. You're addicted to it.

Eventually, people around you will begin giving up. They can't watch anymore. They can't help anymore. Before too long, you find yourself alone. Still digging. Getting even deeper. Until one day you look up, and you can't even see daylight anymore. Just a pinprick of light far, far above. There you are, surrounded by darkness. You are truly lost. All you know is your shovel.

That's when it happens. You are finally ready, and you call for help.

Someone jumps down into the hole with you.

They are not a well-meaning family member. They are not a friend. They are not a coworker. They are not any of the people who have watched you self-destruct for years. In fact, it is probably someone you have never met before in your life: a stranger. Maybe not even a professional. Who they are is a fellow addict.

They smile and say:

"Friend, I've been down here before, and I know the way out. Follow me."

That's true fellowship. That's *suhba*. That's what saved my life—and still saves it today.

Because sometimes the only person who can reach you is someone who's been where you are. Not a philosopher. Not a preacher. But a man with dirt still under his nails. Someone who can say, "I know the way out because I crawled out myself."

That's the miracle of recovery. That's the power of connection. And that's why we don't do this alone.

The first word of the first step is WE.

Understanding True Power and Powerlessness

Power is the ability to influence reality. Starting with your own. It's not volume or muscle. It's not how loud you can yell, or how many people you can control. It's being able to choose your actions and actually follow through. It's when your intentions and behavior match. Genuine power looks like integrity, not domination.

Powerlessness, in contrast, is when the will breaks. It's not weakness or softness; it's when your own self stops responding to you. You want to do right; you make promises, but your hands no longer obey. You tell yourself to stop; you mean it, but you can't. And deep down, you know this truth, though you've avoided speaking it aloud, fearing the collapse of the lie that sustains you.

Addiction feeds on this lie of control, hollowing you out with an endless, insatiable appetite. One is too many, and a thousand is never enough. We are caught in the grip, the phenomenon of craving chasing satisfaction that will never be realized.

You believe you're choosing to use, but in reality, you're obeying. The craving calls, and you answer. The bottle whispers, and your hand moves. You're a slave to your desire.

The moment we start, we're in free fall. We cannot control, moderate, taper, or stop. Yet, we tell ourselves we can. That's addiction's most dangerous lie: "I've got this." We were defeated from the first sip.

That's why admission matters. Step One is a spiritual awakening unto itself. The first crack in the illusion. It's when we stop pretending to be captains and admit we're passengers in a storm we can't navigate.

"We admitted we were powerless over alcohol and that our lives had become unmanageable."

This sentence strikes a death blow to the ego. For many, it's the first truth spoken in years.

It seems paradoxical: surrender to win? Give up to get free? But that's precisely what this Step demands. No half-measures. No damage control. Just raw clarity: "I cannot control this."

Addiction wants everything, not moderation. It's a fire consuming without heat, a hunger devouring without fullness. If you're waiting to feel satisfied, if you think just one more will finally do it, you're already lost. The system is rigged. The house always wins.

But not today.

Today, clarity breaks through. You make the admission. The game breaks, the spell cracks, and Divine Mercy pierces the darkness of self-deception. The war might finally be over.

> "Try not to resist the changes that come your way. Instead, let life live through you. For life is not happening to you. It is responding to you."
>
> Widely attributed to Rumi

Collapse opens the door to a transformation. Step One invites us to stop resisting and start listening to what Allah is trying to teach through pain.

It's a moment so thin you could miss it. But in that frame of time, something cuts through the fog. You see, the truth; not the lies, not the mask, but the wreckage.

In that moment, you reclaim just one sliver of sovereignty, not to control the addiction, but to make an honest decision about it. Not to conquer your broken will, but to admit it's broken. That moment of clarity is grace. Not something you summoned, but Allah's Will moving in. The Almighty granting you an opportunity to change course, Divine light cutting through the fog of an addict's life.

That crack in your heart is mercy. It's Allah creating an opening in a heart sealed by shame and self-will. Through this minor breach, His light illuminates what was hidden.

"My life is unmanageable."

From this place of absolute devastation, everything becomes possible. Not fixed or solved, but possible. Because you finally stop trying to be God and start allowing God to reach you. It's Allah cracking the seal on a heart locked behind shame, delusion, and self-will. It's not dramatic or cinematic. It's usually ugly, quiet, filthy, and humiliating.

But it's real.

And from that crack, if we're willing, we can finally see it: a life in shambles.

The Raw Reality of Unmanageability

What does unmanageability really mean?

It's not philosophical. It's practical and raw, and in your face. Bills unpaid. Jobs lost. Your child's lunch money turned into a bottle. Neglected responsibilities. Running out of people to lie to, yet still lying to yourself.

Unmanageability is chaos becoming your baseline. It's waking in your own filth and wondering how you got there. Again. It's losing jobs, friends, and dignity while telling yourself you're just "going through a rough patch." It's loved ones crying on the phone. It's the look from your boss. It's the neglected dishes rotting in the sink. It's missed court dates and absent birthdays.

It's needing a fix just to feel normal. Because at this point, you don't even get high anymore. You are using just to function. And the deeper you go, the darker your life gets. You hide in that darkness from calls, mirrors, God, and the people who once loved you before you burned them out. You make promises forgotten by morning. You are no longer living; you are merely existing. And barely even doing that.

Unmanageability is living like a ghost in your own life. A specter haunting the ruins of who you used to be.

It's waking on an unfamiliar floor, in clothes you didn't put on, with inexplicable wounds. It's checking your phone with dread; texts, missed calls, incoherent messages you don't recall sending.

It's psychiatric ward collapses. It's losing teeth in pointless fights. It's vomiting in parking lots at 3 a.m. thinking, "I can quit anytime I want."

That's the lie.

You are still believing you can handle it when it has already handled you.

And the moment you admit this truth, even in a whisper or thought, the house of cards collapses. Strangely, that brings relief. You're no longer pretending. It's humiliating, yet holy. The second you admit you're not in control is when you stop playing God, and you let God in.

> *"Allah is the Light of the heavens and the earth."*
>
> (Qur'an, 24:35)

That's Step One: creating a space for the Divine to enter.

We're letting go of the wheel, finally realizing it's not connected to anything. We're done steering into traffic and calling it driving.

We're done calling slavery freedom.

> *"Have you seen the one who takes his desires as his god? And Allah leaves him astray knowingly, and seals his hearing and his heart, and places a*

veil over his sight. So who will guide him after Allah? Will you not then reflect?"

(Qur'an, 45:23)

That was me. That's us. We didn't just follow desires. We worshiped them. We bowed to the bottle, the needle, the lie. We let the *nafs* take the throne, resulting not in freedom but in blindness, deafness, and veiled, diseased hearts.

But the beautiful, terrifying truth is this:

No one can guide us but Allah.

Once you admit the mess, once you stop pretending you're in charge, a strange thing happens. You want guidance. You hope that maybe something greater than your chaos exists. Something greater than your ego. Something that can help you find your way home.

The Commanding Self — Ego and the *Nafs al-Ammāra*

In Islam, the self, called *nafs,* is the part of you that says "me." It's your ego, your cravings, and your pride. The first station, the lowest form of self, is *nafs al-ammāra*, the commanding self. The part that issues orders, saying, "I want that. I deserve that. I don't care who it hurts." It doesn't negotiate but demands. It is the part of you that wants what it wants, when it wants it.

Islam names it clearly: *"Indeed, the soul is a persistent enjoiner of evil..."* (Qur'an, 12:53)

This is the part of us that uses people. That lies and manipulates. That gets high while neglecting responsibilities. That steals from loved ones and dismisses their reactions. That makes excuses for everything and takes responsibility for nothing.

> "The root of every disobedience, indifference, and passion is the satisfaction of the ego."
>
> Attributed to Imam Abu Hamid al-Ghazali

The *nafs al-ammāra* commands through cravings and delusions. When we serve it, we fall into chaos. Step One begins when we admit the ego is not a trustworthy guide.

Real recovery starts with rebellion.

So, when we say, "We admitted we were powerless over alcohol," what we're really saying is:

"I can't listen to that voice anymore. It's been running my life, and it's run it into the ground. The time for rebellion is now."

And that's when something greater can finally begin.

Now, let's examine the rest of the verse:

> "Indeed, the soul is a persistent enjoiner of evil, except for those upon whom my Lord has mercy."

> (Qur'an, 12:53)

That Mercy is what we call a *moment of clarity*.

It's not random or just hitting bottom. Plenty hit bottom and keep digging. But occasionally, if Allah wills, the lights flicker on. For a second, you see what you've become. How far you've fallen. What you've done. And, more terrifyingly, what you can do again.

Once you feel that mercy breaking through, you can't unsee it. You've tasted something real. That's the beginning of a spiritual awakening. Not a thunderbolt, just a breath. Just the first "no" to the commanding self. Just enough light to realize the darkness was never normal.

And mercy is the chisel.

My life didn't become unmanageable because of bad luck. It wasn't a mystery or a curse. It was me. My selfish conduct dragged my life into that deep, deep hole. One selfish and poor decision at a time.

I wasn't a victim. I was the problem.

I lied to those who loved me. I stole from those who trusted me. I used people like tools. If you were close to me, you were disposable. If you had boundaries, I pushed them. If you had faith in me, I abused it. And I did it all while telling myself I was the one getting hurt.

That's what addiction does. But honestly, it wasn't just the substance abuse. I was selfish long before the first drink ever touched my lips. Addiction just opened the door to act on it more recklessly, openly, and destructively. Slavery to my own selfish desires.

Total spiritual chaos. A complete collapse of character. I didn't lose control of my life because I was too sensitive, broken, or misunderstood.

I lost control because I did not know *adab*.

Adab is a profound concept in Islamic spirituality and is absolutely pivotal on the road to recovery. You will see it mentioned many times in this book.

It means how you conduct yourself in the presence of Allah. It is how you speak, act, and move through the world. It is about being in alignment with truth, humility, and grace.

Adab is integrity in motion. It's choosing what's right over what feels good. And when *adab* disappears, everything else follows.

Without *adab*, prayer becomes a performance. Relationships become transactions. Blessings become entitlement. Indulgence becomes addiction. And the self becomes a god.

Reflection Questions – Step One

1. In what ways has my life become unmanageable, and what have been the deeper spiritual consequences?

2. What illusions of control have I clung to, and what would it look like to let go of them?

3. How do I understand surrender as a sacred opening to something greater?

Step One begins the inward turn. It exposes the futility of self-will and invites us to surrender in recognition of a deeper truth. This is where the journey begins: with honesty, humility, and the willingness to let go.

Chapter Two

Waking Up

We are invited to question our old assumptions about God and even reality itself. For many, this is where the fog lifts. Step One showed us that our way isn't working, and now maybe, just maybe, there's another way. This chapter explores the shift from despair to hope, from isolation to connection, and from self-reliance to trust in something greater. In Islamic terms, it's the beginning of *tawakkul,* reliance on Allah and the slow awakening of the *fitrah*, our innate orientation toward the Divine.

Step Two: "Came to believe that a Power greater than ourselves could restore us to sanity."

Big Book of Alcoholics Anonymous (4th Edition):

- "Lack of power, that was our dilemma. We had to find a power by which we could live, and it had to be a Power greater than ourselves." — p. 45

- "Do I now believe, or am I even willing to believe, that there is a Power greater than myself? As soon as a man can say that he does believe, or is willing to believe, we emphatically assure him that he is on his way." — p. 47

Twelve Steps and Twelve Traditions:

- "Step Two is the rallying point for all of us. Whether agnostic, atheist, or former believer, we stand together on this Step." — p. 28

Qur'anic References:

"And whoever puts their trust in Allah — then He is sufficient for them." — (Qur'an, 65:3)

"Say, O My servants who have transgressed against themselves: Do not despair of the mercy of Allah." — (Qur'an, 39:53)

Step Two is the miracle step. Not because belief suddenly makes everything okay, but because it cracks open the possibility that it could be okay someday. That what's been lost might still be restored maybe not perfectly, but certainly meaningfully.

"We came to believe..." and not all at once. Nothing flashy; we did it gradually. We came to just a bit at a time, like waking up from a coma. Slowly. Stiffly. Groggily. But we started.

Gradual belief is a well-known Islamic concept famously echoed in Hadith Qudsi.

> *"If My servant draws near to Me by a handspan, I draw near to him by an arm's length. If he draws near to Me by an arm's length, I draw near to him by a fathom's length. And if he comes to Me walking, I go to him running."*
> The Prophet Muhammad (SAW), Sahih al-Bukhari, 7405

All it takes is the slightest breath of belief, and Allah will move in your life.

Nothing Changes if Nothing Changes

Step One exposed the insanity. It held up a mirror to our chaos and said, "This is where self-will has taken you." Step Two doesn't deny that reality, just re frames it, suggesting that sanity is still possible.

Addiction is deeper than just inappropriate behavior or poor choices. It's a kind of madness. We don't keep using because it's fun. We use because we're caught in a loop we can't break. A loop where the outcome never changes, yet we do it anyway.

One of my sponsor's favorite lines is:

"Insanity is doing the same thing over and over again and expecting different results."

This is more than just a clever quip; it's a diagnosis.

During my time in active addiction, I tried everything to manage my drinking. Whether it was doing a couple of bumps to keep the party going, smoking weed before I went out so I wouldn't drink as much, or drinking on an empty stomach to get drunk faster. I was cultivating better and more efficient methods of insanity. I had it down to a science.

Who does that? Crazy people. My mind was gone.

And Step One made that undeniable. But Step Two asks something even deeper: Can you believe that there's a way back to sanity?

Not to who you were before your first drink. Not to some Instagram-perfect version of yourself. But to real sanity. To clarity. To spiritual balance.

"Restore us to sanity..."

What does that even mean?

Simply put sanity means function, alignment, the restoration of your heart's ability to live purposefully. To know truth from delusion. To feel pain with no need to run from it. To live like your life actually matters again.

> *"Indeed, Allah does not change the condition of a people until they change what is within themselves."*
>
> Qur'an, 13:11

The restoration begins the second we come to believe. A gradual reawakening of the part of you that knows how to stand again. That remembers who carried you when you couldn't.

Accepting Life on Life's Terms

Step Two isn't about theology. It's about beginning to accept reality on reality's terms.

Recovery circles often use the phrase "life on life's terms," and for good reason. It cuts to the core of what sobriety really demands. We're not promised a perfect life. We're not promised fairness. What we're promised is that we'll be sane enough to face life's challenges and joys with equal steadiness. That we'll be able to stay upright in the storm instead of getting drunk over the forecast.

Sanity is having a stable foundation when the earthquakes of life hit. Not freedom from the shaking, but having something solid to hold onto.

Here is the beginning of spiritual resilience.

> *"Do the people think that they will be left to say, 'We believe,' and they will not be tested?"*
>
> Qur'an, 29:2

Life on life's terms means you don't crumble the moment hardship hits. It means you expect the test. And instead of reaching for your old standbys of substances, lies, and self-pity; you reach for God.

This is where recovery and Islam stand shoulder-to-shoulder.

The Qur'an reminds us that hardship is part of the deal. Tests will come. And our job is not to dodge them, but to meet them with trust and integrity.

> *"And We will surely test you with something of fear and hunger and a loss of wealth and lives and fruits, but give good tidings to the patient..."*
>
> Qur'an, 2:155

Step Two invites us to stop fighting against what is and, instead, align with what *could be* through divine restoration. To accept that we are not in control, but that we are still cared for.

In Islamic tradition, this is called *tawakkul.* Trusting in Allah's plan while still showing up for your part. Not passive surrender. Active reliance.

> *"And whoever relies upon Allah—then He is sufficient for him."*
>
> Qur'an, 65:3

We're not called to understand every turn. We're called to walk it with faith. Sanity is regained not by mastering life, but by trusting the One who already wrote it. For years, I trusted the bottle to fix me. In Step Two, I began trusting in Allah's mercy instead. Just a flicker, but enough to feel I could breathe again. We're not called to understand every turn; we are just called to make the turn.

Return to *Fitrah*

> "If you're an apple, you can be the best apple you can be, but you can never be an orange." I was an apple all right, and for the first time I understood that I had spent my life trying to be an orange.
>
> Alcoholics Anonymous, "Window of Opportunity," p. 427

That passage hit me like lightning. I had spent years trying to be an orange. Masking and trying to blend in, pretending I didn't have this thing inside me. Not just alcoholism, but the deeper disease: a complete rejection of my real self.

I wasn't just trying to adapt. I was trying to disappear.

But Step Two isn't about becoming something we're not—it's about being restored to what we truly are beneath the addiction. It asks us to become who we already are. Under the dysfunction. Under the addiction. Under the rot, and rust, and fear.

This is what the Islamic tradition calls *fitrah*—the original, God-given nature of the soul. The state of clarity and harmony that addiction tries to bury. Recovery isn't about growing a new heart. It's about returning to what we were before the corrosion set in.

> *"So direct your face toward the religion, inclining to truth. [Adhere to] the fitrah of Allah upon which He has created [all] people. No change should there be in the creation of Allah."*
>
> Qur'an, 30:30

You weren't born an addict. You weren't born in despair. You were born with light in your chest and mercy woven into your essence. Addiction covered that truth with trauma, fear, and the illusion of control.

Step Two is about returning.

Return to the *fitrah*. Open your heart and return to Allah.

An old timer once told me: "Once a cucumber becomes a pickle, it never becomes a cucumber again..." And that's true. We don't go back to who we were before addiction. But the rest of that saying holds the hope: "...but you can put it in a different jar."

That's Step Two. We're not going back to some innocent state. We're not pretending the wreckage didn't happen. But we're getting moved. Shifted. Cleaned. Placed into something new. Not because we're cured—but because we're actually making some progress.

That's the restoration. Not reversal—repurposing.

The Power of Willingness

Step Two happens before certainty; it's the dawn of faith—it's about direction.

Not even a declaration of virtue—but the turning of the face. Not full belief—just the willingness to believe.

> "As soon as a man can say that he does believe, or is willing to believe, we emphatically assure him that he is on his way."
>
> Alcoholics Anonymous, p. 47

This is the profound invitation of Step Two—that the smallest movement toward belief is met with a divine response far beyond our effort. That's the motion we're invited into—not because Allah needs us to take the step, but because we need Him. He is free of all needs. We are the ones who are lost without Him.

Coming to believe isn't about inventing God. It's about remembering that we've never taken a breath without Him. That the One who formed us in the womb still sees us in the wreckage. That the One who created the *fitrah* never stopped calling us back to it.

Step Two encourages us to remember.

This second step marks our turn from despair to possibility, from isolation to connection. It is the bridge between powerlessness and action—the willingness that opens the door to transformation. We're restoring it, not replacing it with something entirely different. It's remembrance. Here is where hope is born. The words of our spiritual ancestors guide us toward that hope, echoing this willingness to believe.

Reflection Questions – Step Two

1. What does "sanity" mean to me today, and how does it differ from the thinking I had in active addiction?

2. How has my belief in a Power greater than myself begun to take shape, even if imperfectly?

3. What are the barriers—intellectual, emotional, or spiritual—that make it difficult for me to trust in something beyond myself?

The New Path

The moment we admit the possibility that something Greater can restore us, we move differently. We stop folding at the first sign of hardship. We stop hiding from prayer. We stop running from the parts of ourselves we thought were untouchable.

We don't need to know how healing will happen. We just have to stop insisting that it won't.

Despair says, "It's over." Step Two says, "We are just getting started."

And we are on our Way.

Chapter Three

Step Aside

Following the Will of God is like riding on a ship. The ship has its course already laid out and is well underway. Step three merely realizes that we are already doing the Will of Allah whether we realize it. Whether we even want to. Everyone and everything is subject to Divine will—our *qadr*, or Divine decree. *Qadr* is the ship carrying us through life's journey, determining how long we will live, who we will marry, how many children we'll have, and even how many halal corn dogs we'll eat.

You can try to exercise your own will all you want—run around on the deck, sprint from bow to stern to try moving in the opposite direction, shout at the sky, sit in the corner and cry. You can try to bargain, bribe, even threaten—but it all amounts to nothing. The ship is going exactly where Allah wills it. Having admitted our powerlessness in Step One and come to believe in a Higher Power in Step Two, Step Three now invites us to let go of the wheel, surrendering our will to the Creator's course.

Step Three: "Made a decision to turn our will and our lives over to the care of God as we understood Him."

Big Book of Alcoholics Anonymous (4th Edition):

- "The first requirement is that we be convinced that any life run on self-will can hardly be a success." — p. 60

- "Next, we decided that hereafter in this drama of life, God was going to be our Director." — p. 62

Twelve Steps and Twelve Traditions:

- "Practicing Step Three is like the opening of a door which to all appearances is still closed and locked. All we need is a key, and the decision to swing the door open." — p. 34

- "The effectiveness of the whole AA program will rest upon how well and earnestly we have tried to come to 'a decision to turn our will and our lives over to the care of God as we understood Him.'" — p. 35

- "We trust infinite God rather than our finite selves." — p. 37

Qur'anic Reference:
"But you cannot will unless Allah wills. Indeed, Allah is ever Knowing and Wise."
(Qur'an, 76:30)

Turning the Corner

We've moved past Step Two. This is where the ego breaks down. Step Three is decision time.

Understanding *qadr*, that everything happens by the decree of Allah, can be humbling. But it's not defeat. That's where *rida* comes in: the inner state of being content with what Allah has written. It's not resignation. It's peace. When the storms come, or when they pass, you're not demanding life follow your plan. You're trusting the One who crafted The Plan.

> "And acceptance is the answer to all my problems today. When I am disturbed, it is because I find some person, place, thing, or situation—some fact of my life—unacceptable to me, and I can find no serenity until I accept that person, place, thing, or situation as being exactly the way it is supposed to be at this moment. Nothing, absolutely nothing, happens in God's world by mistake. Until I could accept my alcoholism, I could not stay sober; unless I accept life completely on life's terms, I cannot be happy. I need to concentrate not so much on what needs to be changed in the world as on what needs to be changed in me and in my attitudes."
>
> Alcoholics Anonymous, p. 417

The great spiritual teachers say that *rida* isn't passive. It's a joyful surrender. It's the heart saying: "Even this is mercy." Even the pain. Even the detour. Even the wreckage I crawled through to get here.

The Qur'an describes the believers like this:

> *"Allah is pleased with them, and they are pleased with Him."*
>
> Qur'an, 98:8

That's *rida*: mutual contentment. The heart at peace because it's stopped arguing with reality.

Step Three becomes more than just turning things over—it becomes **the doorway into peace.** You stop trying to steer the ship. You trust The One who blows the wind.

A deep, internal shift. In AA, it's "God as you understand Him." In Islam, it's Allah. Same surrender. Same freedom.

> *"The one who surrenders to Allah is truly free."*
>
> Attributed to Imam Ali (ra)

That's the trade: you don't lose yourself. You lose the chains of the self.

The Inner Action of Step Three

Step Three is often called the first true action step, but if you pay attention, the Big Book doesn't place it in the chapter titled Into Action. Instead, it shows up in How It Works. That's not a mistake. The action of Step Three isn't external. It's *completely internal*. This step isn't about doing—it's about deciding. The only action is simply a pivot of the will.

In Islam, this kind of inner transformation is not just familiar—it's foundational. The Arabic word *niyyah* means intention.

> *"Actions are but by intentions, and every man shall have that which he intended."*
>
> The Prophet Muhammad (SAW), Forty Hadith of Imam an-Nawawi #1

The difference between Step Two and Step Three is crucial. Step Two brings you to believe—to seeing that a Power greater than yourself can restore you to sanity. But belief alone doesn't move mountains. Step Three is where you decide to let that Power work in your life. The decision to surrender precedes the act of surrender. That's Step Three. You're not yet moving your body, but you're preparing your soul to hand over the wheel. Even if whispered, the declaration is real: "I'm not the pilot anymore."

God is the source of life. Surrender is sacred. Letting go is how we align with His will. True strength lies in releasing control and allowing His power to move through us.

"You may be in a condition that appears to be a retreat, but in reality, it is an advance. You are being drawn in."
Commonly attributed to Ibn ʿAṭāʾ Allāh al-Iskandarī; (source unverified)

That's Step Three. An inner movement toward God. A holy transaction that happens below the surface, where your will finally bows to something higher.

The Big Book reinforces this truth:

"Next, we decided that hereafter in this drama of life, God was going to be our Director. He is the Principal; we are His agents."
Alcoholics Anonymous, p. 62

This is pure *taslīm*. Not just surrender to God's will, but the offering of oneself into it. Not just asking for help, but for transformation: build with me, do with me.

The Muslim: One Who Submits

So, what does it actually mean to "turn your will and your life over"? It means surrender; it means Islam. The word Islam literally means surrender. A Muslim is one who submits to Divine will, accepts the *qadr*, and trusts in their *rizq*.

A Muslim is, by definition, one who submits their will to Allah. "Islam" means surrender. "Muslim" shares its root with salaam (peace) and *taslīm* (submission). To be Muslim is to surrender the illusion of control and say, "You are the Director. I am Your agent."

"A Muslim is the one from whose tongue and hand the people are safe, and a believer is the one whom the people trust with their lives and wealth."
The Prophet Muhammad (SAW), Sunan an-Nasa'i

True Islam is far beyond mere belief—it's *action rooted in trust*. In recovery, that action begins with a heart decision that sounds a lot like faith: "I can't do this alone. I give it to God."

He also said:

"None of you will truly believe until his desires are in accordance with what I have brought."

Prophet Muhammad (SAW), Forty Hadith of An-Nawawi #41

That's Step Three: *alignment of desire with Divine will.* You don't give up your will entirely—that's not possible. You align it. In recovery and in life, **alignment is the assignment.**

Being Muslim is not about groveling or erasing yourself. It's about recognizing your proper place in the Divine order. You maintain your dignity, your worth, your unique personality—but you stop pretending to be the author of your own life. You become an agent rather than a principal, a servant rather than a master. Remember **EGO = Easing God Out.**

That surrender is uncoerced. It's a choice. That's what makes it powerful. That's what makes it sacred. It's the same choice offered in Step Three. To step away from self-will and entrust your life to The One who was already guiding it all along.

This submission is more than just a belief—it's a practice that transforms how we live and recover.

Servitude and the Path to True Freedom

In the Third Step Prayer, we say:

"Relieve me of the bondage of self, that I may better do Thy will."

Alcoholics Anonymous, p. 63

Remember, we were, and still can be, slaves to our impulses. The *nafs* demanded instant relief. The mind schemed the next fix. The addict dismissed recovery advice with, "I know better." Our cravings. Our pride. Our plans. Addiction didn't just ensnare us—we trapped ourselves.

Even the Prophet Muhammad (SAW) sought refuge from the pull of the self, despite being protected from sin and guided by revelation. He would regularly supplicate:

"O Allah, I seek refuge in You from the evil of my hearing, from the evil
of my sight, from the evil of my tongue, from the evil of my heart, and
from the evil of my desires."

Prophet Muhammad (SAW), Sunan Abu Dawood, 1551

This was Divine awareness. The Prophet (SAW) knew that the self contains both light and shadow. He modeled what it means to turn to Allah not just in hardship, but in vigilance—recognizing that even the most subtle inner distortions can pull us away from the path. If he asked to be protected from himself, how much more should we?

Even when no one else was chasing us, we were running. Even when we had what we thought we wanted, we were restless. That's the bondage of self.

The Qur'an puts it plainly:

"Have you seen the one who takes his own desires as his god?"

Qur'an, 45:23

That's what AA calls "self-will run riot." And it's not freedom—it's delusion. Islam teaches we are always in servitude. The only question is: to what? Either we serve our lower self or we serve Allah. There is no neutral ground.

"Servitude is a gem whose essence is lordship."

Imam Ali ibn Abi Talib (ra), Nahj al-Balagha, Hikmah 252

This single line captures the spiritual reality at the heart of both recovery and Islam. To serve Allah is to step into your highest dignity. It is to align with your true nature—your fitrah—and live under the guidance of The One who knows you better than you know yourself. Servitude to Allah is the path to clarity, peace, and strength. It is where the chaos quiets, the ego softens, and the heart breathes. Step Three calls us into this alignment—into the freedom that comes from faith.

So, when we talk about being "relieved of the bondage of self," what we really mean is choosing whom we serve. We're not giving up the will entirely—we're aligning it with something greater. We fire the false god of the ego. We surrender the fantasy of control. We turn toward the mercy of Allah and say:

"I don't want to run the show anymore. I'm ready to be free."

We find true freedom not in denying servitude, but in choosing the right Master. We stop running against the wind. We turn our faces toward it, and we step with the rhythm of mercy.

This is Step Three in motion. Rather than blind submission, it's a conscious alignment. The decision to trust. To hand over the reins to a Power greater than ourselves and finally live free.

The Discipline of *Sabr*: Steadfast Patience

Step Three is the step where we finally say, "Not my will, but Yours." But that decision doesn't just rewire our spiritual direction—it transforms how we navigate life's challenges. Because turning our will and life over to God means letting go of the addict's need for instant gratification. The transformation eliminates the old "I want what I want when I want it" mindset because the former self no longer exists. And that means learning *sabr*.

Sabr is not merely passive waiting. Nor are we white-knuckling our way through hardship. In the Islamic tradition, *sabr* is steadfast, intentional patience rooted in trust. It's the ability to hold your seat through the storm because you believe the Captain knows where He's taking you. It's the strength to delay comfort for the sake of something higher. It's not denial of suffering—it's the elevation of your response to it.

In active addiction, we bowed to impulse. We worshiped urgency. We couldn't imagine not getting what we wanted right now. In recovery and in Islam, we sacrifice that urgency at the altar of patience. We say: "Even if I don't see it yet, I trust God has something better for me."

> *"Indeed, the patient will be given their reward without measure."*
>
> Qur'an, 39:10

Sabr is the discipline that sustains Step Three. It's what allows the heart to rest, even when the hands are still empty. And it's not without its fruits. The Big Book promises that if we stay the course:

> "We will comprehend the word serenity and we will know peace."
>
> Alcoholics Anonymous, p. 83

That is the reward of *sabr*. That is the path of *rida*. That is the freedom we've been chasing all along—not the freedom to have what we want, but the peace of no longer needing it to be any way but Allah's.

In recovery, this means trusting that sobriety and healing will come in God's time, not ours, even when cravings or doubts feel overwhelming.

Reflection Questions – Step Three

1. What does it mean for me to turn my will over to Allah, and how does that challenge my old patterns of control?

2. Where in my life am I still holding on too tightly, and what would it take to truly surrender those areas?

3. How do I distinguish between passive resignation and active, intentional trust in Divine guidance?

Time to Act

Step Three is the turning point. It affirms our trust in Allah and places our will under His care, not as a retreat, but as an act of courage. This commitment sets the stage for real transformation. Step Four builds on that foundation by calling us to examine our lives with honesty and precision. It is a spiritual inventory—a searchlight turned inward, not to shame, but to understand. If Step Three is the handover, Step Four is the unveiling.

Chapter Four

Sacred Reckoning

I f Step Three was about turning our will over to Allah, then Step Four is about clearing the wreckage that kept us from doing that from the start. More than just a list of incidents, it's a comprehensive moral inventory. A deep look at how addiction and self-centered living warped our sense of right and wrong.

Because most of us lost more than direction, we lost our compass. In active addiction, we justified, minimized, and rationalized. We called survival "strength," manipulation "charm," and harm "just part of the game." Over time, our entire moral framework bent around the need to feed the ego or numb the pain. We stopped asking, "Is this right?" and started asking, "Can I get away with it?"

But now we've taken Step Three. We've turned our lives toward Allah. And if we're serious about doing His will, we have to identify the parts of ourselves that will no longer do. Traits and patterns that once helped us survive may now stand in the way of sincere submission. Step Four is the moment we bring those into the light.

In Islamic tradition, this work is called *muhasaba*—spiritual self-accounting. It's not about shame; it's about clarity. It means taking honest stock of what we did, yes—but also who we became. We examine our resentments, fears, and relationships to uncover patterns and begin taking responsibility. We trace the lies we told ourselves, the principles we violated, and the ways our egos distorted reality. And we do it not just to confess, but to align. If we want to walk the path of surrender, we have to see what pulled us off of it.

Step 4: Made a searching and fearless moral inventory of ourselves.

Big Book of Alcoholics Anonymous (4th Edition):

- "Next we launched out on a course of vigorous action, the first step of which is a personal housecleaning, which many of us had never attempted." — p. 63

- "Resentment is the 'number one' offender. It destroys more alcoholics than anything else." — p. 64

- "We reviewed our fears thoroughly. We put them on paper, even though we had no resentment in connection with them." — p. 68

- "We subjected each relation to this test—was it selfish or not?" — p. 69

Twelve Steps and Twelve Traditions:

- "Creation gave us instincts for a purpose. Without them we wouldn't be complete human beings... Yet these instincts, so necessary for our existence, often far exceed their proper functions." — p. 42

- "We need to examine, carefully and honestly, just what harm we have done others." — p. 52

- "We have to do exactly the opposite. We have to take a hard look at the things within ourselves which had been keeping us sore, and make a rigorous inventory of them." — p. 47

Qur'anic Reference:

"And [by] the soul and He who proportioned it, And inspired it [with discernment of] its wickedness and its righteousness, He has succeeded who purifies it," (Qur'an, 91:8–10)

Vigorous Action

The Big Book puts it simply: "Made a searching and fearless moral inventory of ourselves."

Simple? Maybe. But it can difficult. As addicts we are masters of overcomplication.

Since most of us have spent a lifetime avoiding ourselves and this step means we can no longer escape who were are, we have to face some uncomfortable truths. Even the word "moral" used to make me squirm, but we can no longer skip away. For anyone who's lived in addiction, morality gets stretched—bent to suit survival. And once addiction takes hold, morality doesn't just bend, it snaps. The person in active addiction may engage in behaviors they would never have considered acceptable before - actions that contradict their core values and harm those around them.

This inventory isn't about being perfect. It's about getting honest. And that kind of honesty hurts—at least at first. But it's a necessary pain. A healing pain. One that leads to the type of surrender we couldn't fake even if we tried.

This step is preparation. This is where we make the move from avoiding the truth to living in it. And not just any truth—our truth. No more sidestepping. No more blaming. No more spiritual bypassing. We will have to get our hands dirty with the filth of our past. But we don't get there by cleaning someone else's house. We start with our own.

In the Islamic tradition, people know this practice as *muhasaba*—the accounting of the self. It's not just an audit of actions, but a reckoning with motives, patterns, and attachments. Ibn 'Arabi, the great mystic and scholar, warned: "Beware of yourself, for you are veiled from yourself by yourself." The ego doesn't just act—it hides. It rationalizes, projects, and distorts. Step Four, like *muhasaba*, is uncovering what the ego would rather leave buried. It's not about condemnation—it's about clarity. And clarity is the beginning of freedom.

> *"The intelligent person is the one who holds himself accountable and works for what comes after death. The foolish person is the one who follows his desires and expects Allah to forgive him."*
>
> Prophet Muhammad (SAW), Jami' at-Tirmidhi, Hadith 2459.

That hits like a ton of bricks. Especially if we've been living in cycles of indulgence, delusion, and spiritual procrastination. This is where we break the cycle. This is where we face what we've been hiding from—not just with guilt, but with God. Be cautious not to take the Mercy of Allah for granted.

The first three steps were internal. They happened in the heart, in the will, in the turning. But Step Four demands action. You can't think your way through this one. You write it out. You face it. You name it. You put it in black and white. This is where we dig deep and let the light shine into places we never wanted to look.

You don't need fancy words. You don't need a theology degree. You just need to be fearless. And by fearless, I don't mean reckless. I mean faithful. Fearless, like trusting that Allah's mercy is bigger than our mistakes. Fearless, like believing that the truth won't destroy you—it will liberate you. Fearless, like understanding that the goal isn't to condemn yourself—it's to reclaim yourself.

"An alcoholic is an egomaniac with an inferiority complex."

AA member Mike K.

Recognizing that this contradiction was my default setting helped me stay honest as I began my inventory. Because what we avoid doesn't disappear—it festers. What we resist, persists.

The Inventory of Resentments

Resentment is called the "number-one offender." That's not an exaggeration. If there's one thing that sabotages growth, poisons relationships, fuels relapse, and corrodes the soul—it's resentment. And yet, most of us carried it like armor. We clung to it. We built entire identities around it.

But Step Four asks us to put it under the microscope.

Who do we resent? Why? What does it effect us? And—most critically—where were we at fault?

This isn't about victim-blaming. Let's be clear on that. This is about ownership. It's about stepping out of the role of passive sufferer and recognizing the power we have, even if we misused it. It's about taking responsibility not just for what happened to us, but for how we responded to it, how we carried it, how we weaponized it, or let it fester.

Before we ever took a drink or a hit, many of us were already deeply resentful. Long before we used, we were harboring pain. Pain we never named. Pain we weren't ready to feel. So we numbed it, resented it, projected it. And eventually, we let it become a part of our identity.

The Pattern of Expectations and Resentments

An expectation is a premeditated resentment.

Let that sink in. Most of the resentments I listed in my Fourth Step had their roots in unspoken, unrealistic, or unfair expectations. I expected people to behave in a certain way. I expected the world to accommodate my needs. I expected to be loved, respected, understood, without ever communicating what I needed. I lived in a constant state of self-induced disappointment.

Why? Because I was trying to control the three things recovery teaches we absolutely cannot control: people, places, and things. Holding all three to impossible standards.

When you expect something that doesn't happen, and you don't let it go—it turns into resentment. It hardens. It becomes poison. And that poison seeps into everything. Relationships. Recovery. Prayer. Joy.

In Islam, resentment is a symptom of deeper diseases: *ghadab* (anger), *ujb* (self-righteousness), and *kibr* (arrogance). These are more than minor character flaws. They are illnesses of the heart.

> *"Do not let the hatred of a people prevent you from being just. Be just: that is nearer to righteousness."*
>
> Qur'an, 5:8

It's not just about whom we resent. It's about how resentment blocks justice, distorts our vision, and keeps us disconnected from the *nur*—the light of Allah.

Sufi wisdom warns us that the ego loves to play the victim because it preserves its illusion of control. When we're the victim, we don't have to change. When we're the victim, we're always justified. But recovery—and Islam—both ask us to go deeper. They ask us to look in the mirror.

Turning Inward

I used to be amazing at taking moral inventory—of other people. I had opinions, judgments, and commentary. I could dissect someone else's character defects with surgical precision. But when it came time to turn that lens inward?

I vanished.

I deflected with jokes. Changed the subject. Blamed someone else. Or just disappeared altogether. The Irish Goodbye wasn't just my party trick—it was my way of life.

But Step Four doesn't let you ghost yourself. It makes you show up. It dares you to sit down with your own story and ask the hard question: what was my role?

That question cracked me wide open. Even when others genuinely wronged me and clearly harmed me, I still had to examine my response. How I carried that harm. How I let it mutate into rage, revenge, manipulation, or pride.

> *"Do you order righteousness of the people and forget yourselves while you recite the Scripture? Then will you not reason?"*
>
> Qur'an, 2:44

Context:

- This verse criticizes hypocrisy, commanding others toward goodness while neglecting one's own spiritual state.

- It's a deep reminder that mere knowledge or preaching is not enough; sincere internal practice is essential.

That was me. Pointing at everyone else.

This step flipped the script. It dared me to stop scanning the horizon for problems and start searching my heart for the truth. And when I did, I realized how much of my anger, my righteous indignation, my outrage, and my moral superiority, was just ego in a costume.

I was angry that people didn't see the world like I did. Angry that they didn't act the way I thought they should. Angry that they weren't angry enough. Or weren't miserable as me.

Misery really does love company.

And when no one joined my pity party, I turned that into fuel. Anger became my weapon. My defense. My drug. Both Islam and recovery programs treat anger as a spiritual disease.

> *A man said to the Prophet (SAW), "Advise me." The Prophet (SAW) said, "Do not get angry." The man repeated his request several times, and each time the Prophet (SAW) replied, "Do not get angry."*
> Prophet Muhammad (SAW), Sahih al-Bukhari 6116

He didn't say, "Don't drink." He didn't say, "Don't fornicate." He said: **Don't get angry.**

Why?

Because anger blinds us. It empowers the *nafs* and makes us feel justified in our delusions. It creates a veil between us and Allah. And when we're consumed by anger, we're consumed by self. The Divine becomes distant—not because Allah has moved, but because we did.

It's not just about managing anger in the moment. That comes later—in Step Ten. Here in Step Four, we're documenting the damage it's already done. We're naming it. Calling it out. Mapping its patterns. Because if we don't see the pattern, we'll keep repeating it.

When I sat down with this section of the inventory, it was overwhelming. The list of people I resented was long. But what cut deeper was seeing the thread that ran through them all—my ego, entitlement, fear, and immaturity.

Resentment did more than hurt—it formed me. And it fueled my addiction and turned me into someone I didn't recognize. Step Four offered something different: a chance to confront what I'd buried and name what had served me but would not serve Allah.

The Inventory of Fears

Fear is the silent architect of a thousand poor decisions. And it's sneakier than most of us want to admit. For many in recovery, fear is the real addiction. We drank to drown it. Used to mute it. Lied to cover it. Manipulated to escape it. We were addicted to control, not just substances, and fear drove that compulsion.

Step Four invites us to look at our fears with clarity and compassion—to avoid self-shame and finally to unmask what has been whispering in our ear for so long. Fear is a liar. It always has been.

The Big Book says we are "driven by a hundred forms of fear." And it's not wrong. Fear of not getting what we want. Fear of losing what we have. Fear of being alone, seen, rejected, or unloved. Fear of being found out. Fear of failure. Fear of success. Fear of being abandoned. Fear of being ordinary. Fear of being extraordinary. Fear of being ourselves.

Fear runs deep. It hides behind ambition, arrogance, judgment, procrastination, and people-pleasing. It's the root of much of our behavior, but most of us have never called it by its name. Until now.

Fear vs. Awe in Islam

In the Islamic tradition, fear is not inherently bad. It's a natural part of the human condition. The Qur'an speaks often of fear—although not the kind that paralyzes. The fear that Allah asks of us is awe. Reverence. Humility in the face of majesty.

> *"Indeed, those who fear their Lord unseen will have forgiveness and a great reward."*
>
> Qur'an, 67:12

This is the kind of fear that purifies the heart—what the scholars call *khawf*. It's the trembling awareness that our actions matter because our connection with Allah matters. It's the fear that draws us closer, that sharpens our conscience and humbles the heart. *Khawf* is the longing to remain near to the Divine, to stay aligned with His mercy, and to avoid anything that would dim that nearness. It's the fear that keeps love honest.

That kind of fear? That's sacred. That's the fear that leads to freedom. Because it reminds you what actually matters.

> *"Your fear of loss comes from your lack of trust in Allah."*
>
> Ibn ʿAṭāʾ Allāh al-Sakandarī, al-Ḥikam Aphorism #42

When I did my fear inventory, I saw just scarcity had shaped much of my life. Fear of not having enough. Not being enough. Not being loved. Not being secure. Fear of failure. Fear of poverty. Fear of humiliation. Fear of being unworthy. Fear of being forgotten.

I was still operating in survival mode—even in sobriety.

Growth in Recovery

Here is a truth: the first time I did my Fourth Step, all my fears were selfish. All of them pointed back to me. My needs. My image. My insecurities. My sense of control.

But after I relapsed and came back, something had changed.

I was a father now. A husband. I had people who depended on me. People I loved. My fears were no longer about my survival. They were about who I hurt when I failed and how hurt they would be if I failed again. And beneath all of that—was a deeper fear.

The fear of disappointing Allah.

That fear wasn't shame-based. It did not stem from punishment. It stemmed from love. And it marked a turning point in my recovery. That Fourth Step wasn't a redo. It was a reawakening.

> *"The heart in its journey to Allah is like a bird. Love is its head, and fear and hope are its two wings."*
>
> Ibn al-Qayyim, Madārij al-Sālikīn

Fear, when rightly placed, is a tool. It's propulsion. It gives us the humility to know we are not in control—and the courage to trust The One who is.

That's *tawakkul.*

> *"And whoever puts their trust in Allah — then He is sufficient for them."*

Qur'an, 65:3

Fear reveals where we still believe Allah is not enough. Where we still think it's on us to fix everything. Where we've mistaken our own control for safety. *Tawakkul* reminds us: you were never supposed to carry it alone.

Let me be real: I still wrestle with fear. I still get tempted to white-knuckle life. But I've learned that fear shrinks when awe of Allah expands.

Questions for Self-Examination

The inventory of fears reveals something surprising: it's a window into what you worship. This connection reveals a link between fear and worship. We give power to what we fear. We submit to it. Obey it. Shape our lives around.

- What have I been worshipping instead of Allah?

- What did I believe could harm me more than Allah could protect me?

- What have I allowed to sit on the throne of my heart?

When I asked myself those questions, I found false gods everywhere. Money. Control. Validation. Reputation. All of them: crumbling idols. And the longer I knelt before them, the more anxious and exhausted I became.

Tawakkul is the great replacement. *Tawakkul* transforms fear to awe. It doesn't deny risk—it acknowledges The One who governs all outcomes.

So, when you make your fear list, go deep. Be specific. Be bold. But don't stop there.

Don't just name what you're afraid of. Ask: **What would trust look like here?**

Because the goal isn't fearlessness. It's faithfulness. And that's what we're really trying to recover—trust. Trust in God. Trust. Trust that the same Power that got you here will continue to work with you.

You don't have to know the outcome. You just have to trust The One who does.

The Inventory of Sex Conduct

While resentments and fears form the core of many inventories, our sexual conduct often carries the heaviest emotional and spiritual weight. This is the part that makes many people hesitate. The section in the Fourth Step even sometimes gets skipped, glossed over, or even left blank. But for many of us, it's the one we most need to face.

Because sex isn't just physical. It's power. It's validation. It's pain. It's longing. It's all the tangled stuff we didn't know how to name—wrapped in a moment of intimacy we often weren't ready for. Or worse, abused.

This isn't about shame. It's about truth. And for many people in recovery, our sexual history is where we hid our deepest wounds and darkest motives. Sometimes, we used sex to connect. Sometimes, we used it to escape. Sometimes, we used it to prove we mattered. And sometimes—to prove we didn't.

> "We subjected each relation to this test—was it selfish or not? We asked
> God to mold our ideals and help us to live up to them."
>
> (Alcoholics Anonymous, p. 69)

That's the work here. Not to relive the past, but to sift through it. Not to drown in guilt, but to separate truth from illusion. Not to shame ourselves, but to learn how to handle this sacred part of our being in a way that reflects who we're becoming—not who we were.

The Body as Sacred Trust

The Islamic lens calls this *amanah*—trust. Our body is not our possession. It's a trust. A gift from Allah. Something we care for, honoring, and using in line with Divine wisdom. That includes our sexual desires.

The Qur'an reminds us that God will not overlook any aspect of our being, as stated:

> *"Indeed, the hearing, the sight, and the heart—each will be questioned."*
>
> Qur'an, 17:36

We are responsible not just for what we do—but for why we do it. For the intention behind the act. Our hearts' condition brought us there.

Cultural and Personal Perspectives

Let's be honest: across many societies, approaches to sexuality vary. In some contexts, it's commodified yet trivialized. In many traditional Muslim communities, it's considered sacred, but cultural norms often limit discussions about it, rather than religious teachings. Those of us in recovery, especially reverts, often navigate these contrasting perspectives.

We know what it's like to use sex for validation, revenge, power, or distraction. We know what it's like to regret what we said, what we did, or who we used. And we know what it's like to wonder if we'll ever be whole again.

> "Everything is about sex except sex. Sex is about power."
> Frank Underwood, House of Cards (fictional character, dialogue often mis-attributed to Oscar Wilde)

This quote, though from a fictional character, captures the misuse of sex as power rather than a sacred connection. So many of our encounters weren't about love, connection, or sacred union. They were about control. Or desperation. Or an attempt to feel something—or nothing.

And for many of us, especially in our darkest moments, sex became another drug. It stopped being about intimacy and became a transaction. A means of escape. A way to manipulate, numb, or forget.

But in Islam, sex isn't dirty. It's Divine. When done within the bounds of marriage, with sincerity, love, and mercy—it's worship. It's a pathway to tranquility.

> *"And among His signs is that He created for you spouses from among yourselves, that you may find tranquility in them. And He placed between you love and mercy."*
>
> Qur'an, 30:21

That's the goal. That's the ideal. But many of us are still carrying the residue of something far from that.

Facing the Truth

Zina, or unlawful sexual contact, is a major sin in Islam. It carries weight because of the spiritual, emotional, and psychological impact of sexual intimacy. Islam treats sex as something sacred—an act that involves the exchange of vulnerability, energy, and deep connection. The boundaries around it preserve that sanctity and protect both the individual and the community.

S.E.X. = Sacred Energy eXchange

In its highest form, it's a bridge between bodies and souls. The literal bridge of life. A moment where heaven and Earth meet. Where vulnerability and trust become one. But outside the container of commitment—outside the boundaries Allah has set—it becomes a distortion. The *nafs* grabs hold, and what was sacred turns into something selfish. Something harmful and ultimately spiritually costly.

When we take inventory here, we're not writing erotica. We're not shaming ourselves. We're naming what it cost us. Not just emotionally—but spiritually. What did we give away that wasn't ours to give? Who did we hurt? What did we ignore?

Questions for Self-Examination

- Did I treat this body as a sacred trust?

- Did I treat someone else's body as if it belonged to me?

- What was I trying to feel—or avoid?

- Did I use sex to escape spiritual discomfort?

Because here's the truth: a lot of us weren't chasing sex—we were chasing something deeper. Belonging. Worth. Connection. Control. Escape. And if we don't understand that now, we'll just carry those patterns into our next relationship, our next mistake, our next spiral.

Islam teaches us to conceal past sins—not to broadcast them, but to reckon with them privately. Step Four is not a public confession. It's not a retelling of your worst memories for shame's sake. It's a spiritual inventory—an honest accounting between you and Allah. This step isn't about punishment. It's about purification.

> *"The one who repents from sin is like one who did not sin."*
> The Prophet Muhammad (SAW), Sunan Ibn Mājah, 4250

That's not metaphor. That's mercy. Sincere *tawbah* means that, through recognition and return, you lift the weight of your past as if it never existed.

But that return begins with recognition. That's why Step Four matters. You're not writing this to release yourself. To release others. To unhook your heart from the shame that's been dragging behind you like a chain. This is a reckoning, not a spectacle. You are confronting your story, patterns, and burdens you were never meant to carry forever.

Reflection Questions – Step Four

1. What patterns do I see in the harms I caused or experienced, and what do they reveal about my character defects?

2. How honest have I truly been in facing the parts of myself I've tried to hide—from others, from God, and from myself?

3. In what ways has this inventory already lightened my heart—or challenged me to grow?

Bringing It All Into the Light

The Fourth Step is preparation. When we complete our inventory, we've done something many people never do in a lifetime: we've faced ourselves honestly. This isn't the end of our journey, but it's where the real transformation begins.

As you work through your inventory, remember that Allah sees you not only as you are, but as you are becoming.

> *"Allah does not look at your appearance or wealth, but rather at your hearts and deeds."*
>
> Prophet Muhammad (SAW), Sahih Muslim 2564

In this step, we align those hearts and deeds—bringing what was hidden into the light to heal it.

Take your time. Be thorough. Be honest. The debris you clear away now makes room for what Allah has always intended for you: a heart at peace, a soul in alignment, and a life of purpose.

With this sacred reckoning complete, Step Five will guide us to share our inventory, releasing its weight to sail toward deeper surrender.

Chapter Five

Unburdened Heart

Afterintense inner work—wrestling with truth, memory, and ego—we've finally laid it all out in Step Four. Not just to vent, but to examine. We've exposed our past patterns, identified the actual sources of harm, and traced the lines of damage that shaped who we became. The lies we told, the fears that drove us, the harm we caused and endured—they're no longer hidden. We've seen ourselves clearly.

But even now, we haven't finished our journey.

Because self-perception is fragile. Sometimes we miss something vital. Sometimes we inflate things that aren't really there. Therefore, you shouldn't take the next step alone. We need another perspective—someone grounded, someone who's walked this path. Not to shame us or solve us, but to witness with clarity and compassion. Someone who can help us confirm what's real and gently challenge what isn't.

Step Five is that moment.

It's not about unloading every detail for the sake of storytelling. It's about sharing the shape of our story—the patterns, the defenses, the weight we carried without even realizing it. We're not seeking punishment. We're seeking perspective. Because if we're going to rebuild a life aligned with truth, we can't do it in isolation.

And something deep inside us is ready to move forward.

Step 5: Admitted to God, to ourselves, and to another human being the exact nature of our wrongs.

Big Book of Alcoholics Anonymous (4th Edition):

- "We may not overcome drinking until we have done our utmost to straighten out the past." — p. 73

- "They had not learned enough of humility, fearlessness and honesty, in the sense we find it necessary, until they told someone else all their life story." — p. 73

- "We pocket our pride and go to it, illuminating every twist of character, every dark cranny of the past." — p. 75

Twelve Steps and Twelve Traditions:

- "This practice of admitting one's defects to another person is of such importance that it occupies a prominent place in our Steps and traditions." — p. 56

- "More than most people, the alcoholic leads a double life." — p. 58

- "Until we let go of our secrets, they fester and rot the soul. But when shared with God and another human being, healing begins." — p. 60

- "Another great dividend we may expect from confiding our defects to another human being is humility..." — p. 58

Qur'anic Reference:

"Allah is the ally of those who believe. He brings them out from darkness into light." (Qur'an, 2:257)

Point of Clarity

Before we go any further, we need to name a tension that will be very real for many Muslims approaching Step Five: the concept of confessing your sins to another person.

Islamic tradition views this as not simply discouraged, but as a violation of the sacred veil Allah has mercifully placed over our past mistakes. The Prophet (SAW) taught us that if Allah has concealed our sins, we should not uncover them, neither in public nor in private conversations. The dignity of the believer is a trust, and exposing one's faults can harm the soul, invite judgment, and open doors that remained closed.

> *"Every one of my followers will be forgiven except those who expose their wrongdoings..."*
>
> Prophet Muhammad (SAW), Sahih al-Bukhari, 6069

So, how do we reconcile this with Step Five?

The answer begins with a careful reading. The Step does not say, "admitted every sin we've ever committed."

It says: "Admitted the exact nature of our wrongs."

That distinction is foundational.

The nature of our wrongs speaks to the deeper patterns, the tendencies of the *nafs*, the emotional undercurrents, the justifications, the cycles we could not seem to break. It is not the act itself, but what the act reveals about the condition of the heart.

In this way, Step Five becomes not a confessional, but a sacred act of *muhasaba*---a deep, courageous self-inventory done in the presence of Allah and shared with a trustworthy guide for the sake of healing and growth. This is not about shame. It is about breaking the spiritual isolation in which addiction thrives. It is about returning to truth.

True Purpose

Many people misunderstand Step Five, especially outside of recovery. The idea of telling another human being about our faults can stir up fear and resistance. It feels like a step backward into humiliation when, in truth, it's a step forward into freedom.

Step Five isn't about punishment. It's not about dredging up every specific mistake. It's about naming the deeper truths. Identifying the patterns that governed our behavior, the character defects that harmed others, and the beliefs that kept us spiritually sick.

It's also about breaking the spell of isolation.

Addiction thrives in secrecy, and it feeds off compartmentalization. The Big Book says that if we skip this step, "we may not overcome drinking." (*Alcoholics Anonymous*, p. 72). Not because talking is magic, but because hiding is the disease.

Step Five is the medicine.

It allows us to say: This is what I've been carrying. This has shaped me. This is what I want to be free from.

For the Muslim, this doesn't require detailing every sin. It means describing the contours of the heart. Was it arrogance? Envy? Lust? Pride? Despair? Fear? These are not private stories. These are universal diseases of the heart. And when we name them aloud, in a way that still honors the veil Allah has placed over our past, we surrender them.

Sharing in a Halal Way

For the Muslim in recovery, Step Five must be done with both courage and *adab* (spiritual etiquette). Islam places a high value on modesty and dignity. We are not to expose what Allah has concealed.

> *"Indeed, those who like to spread immorality among the believers will suffer a painful punishment..."*
>
> Qur'an, 24:19

So, how do we fulfill this step without crossing sacred boundaries?

The key lies in understanding the difference between *nature* and *narrative*.

The *nature* of our wrongs refers to the underlying patterns and character defects—the diseases of the heart. Examples include:

- "I consistently put my desires above others' needs."

- "I manipulated situations for personal gain."

- "I harbored resentments that poisoned my relationships."

- "I allowed fear to control my decisions. "

- "I used people to feed my ego and then discarded them when they no longer served my purpose. "

- "I lived in dishonesty, not just with others but with myself about who I truly was. "

The *narrative* refers to specific details—names, places, explicit descriptions of acts, particularly those involving others. These specifics are best left between you and Allah alone.

This distinction allows us to be profoundly honest about our character while still honoring Islamic principles of dignity and privacy. We're not hiding from accountability—we're channeling it appropriately.

> "Say, 'O My servants who have transgressed against themselves [by sinning], do not despair of the mercy of Allah. Indeed, Allah forgives all sins...'"

> Qur'an, 39:53

"We pocket our pride and go to it, illuminating every twist of character..." (*Alcoholics Anonymous*, p. 75) This supports the Islamic focus on character, not specific sinful acts.

"Another great dividend... is humility." (*Twelve Steps and Twelve Traditions*, p. 58) Humility, not detail, is the goal. That's what breaks the isolation.

Because of this, it is not only possible, it may be spiritually necessary for the Muslim to perform two aspects of Step Five:

1. A spiritual reflection with a guide, focused on the patterns, character defects, and emotional drivers behind our behavior—the nature of our wrongs.

2. A private repentance with Allah, where we can be completely specific, holding nothing back from The One who already knows all.

Choosing Someone to Hear Your Fifth Step

Who should hear your Fifth Step? This is a crucial question, especially for Muslims navigating both recovery and *deen*. The Big Book asks us to admit the exact nature of our wrongs to another human being. Islamic teachings encourage concealing sins, making this type of disclosure delicate. That's why choosing the right person matters.

Ideally, it should be someone who:

- Understands recovery and respects Islamic boundaries

- Can remain objective

- Has taken their own Fifth Step and knows the weight of this process

- Can maintain confidentiality and composure

- Listens with humility, not judgment

- Offers spiritual maturity, not control

This might be a Muslim sponsor, an imam familiar with addiction recovery, a trusted friend on the path, or a counselor who respects your faith. What matters isn't their title—it's their integrity. They must understand that this is not a casual conversation. It's an act of spiritual courage. As the Prophet ☐said:

> *"Consult your heart. Righteousness is what the soul feels at ease with, and sin is what causes discomfort in the soul—even if people approve it."*
> Prophet Muhammad (SAW), Musnad Ahmad 17517; Sunan al-Dārimī
> 2533

If your heart feels at ease, even amid fear, when speaking to this person, they may be the right one.

If You Can't Find the Ideal Person

You may live in a place where it's hard to find someone who meets all these criteria. That doesn't mean Step Five is off the table.

Here are a few adaptations others have found helpful:

- Work with a non-Muslim sponsor or counselor who's open to understanding Islamic values

- Consult with a local imam first about how to approach this step respectfully, then work with a recovery professional

- Reach out to Muslim recovery communities in other areas—support doesn't have to be local to be effective

The goal is to break isolation while protecting dignity. That balance is possible—with sincerity, intention, and prayer.

The Power of Speaking It Aloud

There's a kind of healing that only comes when we speak the truth aloud. Step Five isn't just about writing inventory; it's about naming it in front of another human being and in the presence of Allah. For many of us, this is the first time we've told the whole truth without excuse, performance, or denial. And when the person listening doesn't recoil; when they nod, breathe, and say, "I've been there too"—something shifts.

This is *tawbah*: the act of returning to Allah with full knowledge of our mistakes and a sincere intention to change. Admitting our faults to another helps clear the fog. It humbles us. It grounds us. It prepares us for the next steps on the path. Step Five may be painful—but it is also sacred. And it opens the door to the freedom we forgot was possible.

Reflection Questions—Step Five

1. What emotions arise when I consider speaking my flaws aloud, and what are those emotions trying to protect?

2. Am I more afraid of how others will see me—or how I will see myself in the light of Allah's truth?

3. What would it look like to admit the state of my heart, not just the actions I've taken?

The Bridge to Transformation

We've identified our patterns in Step Four, we've spoken them aloud in Step Five, and now we prepare for the deeper work of transformation that follows.

Our own examination, but in the presence of someone who can see clearly and respond with compassion, has brought into the light, not just our defects. We have named the harmful patterns. The weak spots acknowledged. We've stopped pretending we were fine all along.

That honesty creates readiness. Readiness for what? For change. Genuine change. Not just surface-level improvements, but deep moral and spiritual transformation. The kind that only begins once we stop hiding and start healing.

In the Islamic tradition, *tawba*, repentance, is not just sorrow or guilt. It's return. Return to Allah. Return to our *fitrah*, our pure, original nature. Return to a life of growth and submission. And with the burden of secrecy lifted through Step Five, we're finally light enough to begin that return in earnest.

That's where we go next. Having admitted the exact nature of our wrongs to Allah, to ourselves, and to another human being, we can now ask: Am I ready to let these patterns go? Am I ready for Allah to remove them?

Step Six begins with the truth of that answer.

Chapter Six

Quiet Shift

W e've faced ourselves in Step Four. We've shared what we found in Step Five. We have exposed our patterns, flaws, and damage. And now we arrive at a quiet but crucial turning point in the process of change: preparation.

Before any lasting change can take root, something internal has to shift. Old defenses have to be let go. Self-justification, denial, and pride have to be stripped away. We must clear the heart of what no longer serves, so something new can actually take hold. If we skip this, the rest won't stick. Not for long.

Step Six is that inner preparation. There's nothing to say, nothing to do—not yet. It's invisible. But it's essential. A heart unprepared cannot receive prayer, amends, or service, no matter how much is offered.

This is where we become entirely ready to have Allah remove our defects of character. Not halfway ready. Not conditionally ready. But fully, sincerely, and without holding back.

Step 6: Were entirely ready to have God remove all these defects of character.

Big Book of Alcoholics Anonymous (4th Edition):

- "If we can answer to our satisfaction, we then look at Step Six. We have emphasized willingness as being indispensable." — p. 76

- "If we still cling to something we will not let go, we ask God to help us be willing." — p. 76

Twelve Steps and Twelve Traditions:

- "This is the Step that separates the men from the boys." — p. 63

- "Step Six is the beginning of a lifetime job." — p. 64

- "The only urgent thing is that we make a beginning, and keep trying." — p. 65

Qur'anic Reference:

"The Day when neither wealth nor children will benefit [anyone], but only one who comes to Allah with a sound heart." (Qur'an, 26:88-89)

Step of Solitude

Here is another quiet step, and one of the most powerful. There is no writing. No conversation. No outward act of confession or prayer. You can take Step Six sitting right where you are. It's completely an internal shift, a private act of surrender that no one may see, but Allah does. And if it's sincere, your heart will be ready.

This is where we become entirely ready; not halfway, not most, but fully open, for God to begin the deep work in our hearts. To remove what has hardened. To dissolve what distorts. We will prepare a space within ourselves for something cleaner, softer, and more aligned with our true selves. This is the point where the heart consents to healing.

Symptoms of an Unsound Heart

This is the first step, mentioning character defects. But these defects are not the disease; they are symptoms. Just as a cough signals a deeper illness, sarcasm may be a symptom of arrogance. Lying may stem from fear. Jealousy might reflect insecurity or a lack of trust in Allah's *rizq* (provision).

We could list defects for pages: impatience, resentment, vanity, pride, people-pleasing, harshness, manipulation, perfectionism, martyrdom, and self-pity. But beneath them all lies one spiritual ailment: a diseased heart.

The Big Book says it plainly: "Selfishness---self-centeredness! That, we think, is the root of our troubles" (*Alcoholics Anonymous*, p. 62). Addiction was only the fruit. Self-centered fear, pride, control, and the need to play God, hat was the root system. And our defects were the twisted vines growing from that poisoned soil.

> *"Truly in the body there is a piece of flesh which, if it is sound, the whole body is sound; and if it is corrupt, the whole body is corrupt. Verily, it is the heart"*
> Prophet Muhammad (SAW), Sahih al-Bukhari 52; Sahih Muslim 1599

What we are facing now are the diseases of the heart: arrogance (*kibr*), envy (*hasad*), hatred, heedlessness (*ghaflah*), insincerity (*riya'*), and more. These are the hidden infections that drove our behavior. Step Six is when we stop managing symptoms and start asking for a cure.

Ego Death in Stillness

The Sufis speak of *fana,* the annihilation of the self. Not physical death, but the death of the illusion that we are in control.

Step Three was the decision to turn our will over. Step Six is where that decision becomes real. We inch toward the edge of the diving board, heart pounding, knees shaking, and though we haven't jumped yet (that's Step Seven), we are entirely ready.

No more "I." No more negotiations. No more "This is just who I am."

"Die before you die." This prophetic wisdom, echoed in the Way of Islam, is at the heart of Step Six. This is the beginning of ego death. The stillness before the surrender. And it is sacred ground.

This is an echo of the Second Step. You don't have to be perfect or have it all figured out. You just have to be willing.

> "If we still cling to something we will not let go, we ask God to help us be willing"
>
> Alcoholics Anonymous, p. 76

Step Six isn't about force. It's about alignment. It's about turning your face toward Allah and saying, "I'm done doing surgery on myself. I trust You now."

We do this with sincerity and our hearts open to healing.

Tawba and *Ta'ahub* : Dimensions of Readiness

In Islamic tradition, two spiritual concepts align beautifully with Step Six: *tawba* (repentance) and *ta'ahub* (preparation).

Tawba isn't merely saying "I'm sorry". It's a complete reorientation toward Allah. The root of the word means "to return," suggesting that we aren't becoming something new but returning to our *fitrah*—our natural state. Step Six embodies this return. We aren't trying to become someone else—we're preparing for Allah to restore us to our original selves.

Ta'ahub refers to spiritual preparation—making oneself ready for Divine encounters. Before prayer, we perform *wudu*. Before Ramadan, we prepare our hearts and homes. Before Hajj, we enter *ihram*. Each is a readiness that precedes transformation.

Three Essential Stages of *Tawbah*

1. *I'tirāf* – Recognition and acknowledgment of the sin

2. *Nadam* – Sincere remorse and heartfelt regret

3. *'Azm* – A firm resolution never to return to the sin

Step Six aligns with this third stage. The deep, inner commitment to leave behind what no longer serves our spiritual growth. It's not about immediate perfection. It's about becoming entirely ready. Ready to release the character defects that kept us stuck. Ready to be changed by The One who heals.

When we become "entirely ready," we aren't just checking off another step. We are engaging in a sacred Islamic practice of return and preparation. We are declaring to Allah: "I am ready for You to restore my heart to its original purity, to remove what distances me from You, and to bring me back to the path of *fitrah*."

Practical Steps Toward Readiness

How do we become "entirely ready"? This internal step can feel abstract, but there are practices that can help prepare the heart.

1. Identify the resistance—Which defects are you still defending or rationalizing? Often, these are the ones we've re-framed as strengths or essential parts of our personality. This might include traits like perfectionism that we've convinced ourselves are virtues rather than manifestations of fear and control.

2. Practice spiritual emptying—In daily prayer, practice letting go of control, ambition, and self-definition. Enter *salah* as if nothing matters except your presence before Allah. When you stand for prayer, consciously set aside your worldly identities: your job title, your social status, your achievements, and failures. Let each prostration be a physical embodiment of surrender, where your forehead meets the earth and your heart meets humility. Allow the rhythm of prayer

gradually to soften your attachment to the defects you once clung to.

3. Imagine life without them—For each character defect, ask: "What would my life look like without this trait?" This helps separate your true identity from the behaviors that have become familiar but harmful. Consider how your relationships, spiritual connection, and peace of mind might change if you removed this defect.

4. Remember the pain—Reflect on how these character defects have harmed you and others. This isn't about shame, but honest recognition. Recall specific instances when your arrogance alienated loved ones, or when your fear prevented you from fulfilling your purpose. Let the reality of these consequences strengthen your readiness.

5. Seek Divine support—The Qur'an teaches us to ask Allah for help in purification. Make this request part of your daily *d'ua*, acknowledging that true readiness comes from Allah's help.

"Our Lord, make us Muslims [submitting] to You and from our descendants a Muslim nation [submitting] to You. And show us our rites and accept our repentance. Indeed, You are the Accepting of repentance, the Merciful"

Qur'an, 2:128

Force or perfect understanding does not achieve readiness. It's cultivated through consistent surrender, honest reflection, and the humble acknowledgment that we cannot heal ourselves. Only Allah can transform the heart.

Reflection Questions—Step Six

1. Which character defects do I still cling to, and what false sense of identity or control do they provide?

2. Am I truly ready to let go of these defects, or am I secretly bargaining to keep a few?

3. What would it feel like to trust Allah enough to be changed, even if I don't know who I'll be without these flaws?

Looking Ahead: From Readiness to Action

Preparation is essential, but it isn't the end goal. Once we've done the internal clearing: facing our patterns, letting go of denial, and becoming truly willing, something must come next.

Step Six sets the stage for Step Seven, where readiness becomes action. Where silent willingness becomes spoken prayer. Where we beseech Allah to remove our defects of character.

But without the sincerity of Step Six, that prayer would fall flat. Without full willingness, there can be no real transformation. Surface change without inner consent doesn't last.

That's why this quiet, invisible step carries so much weight. It's the turning point between recognizing what needs to change—and opening ourselves to The One who can actually change it. It's when we stop trying to fix ourselves by force and admit, from the heart, that we're ready to let Allah do what we cannot.

As you move forward, carry this readiness with you. It isn't a one-time realization. It's a spiritual stance: one of openness, trust, and ongoing surrender. The willingness to be changed by Allah is not just for early recovery. It is the posture of a Muslim life: submission to the Divine Will.

In fact, this step is the lived meaning of Islam itself.

Chapter Seven

Quality Control

You sat down and told the truth. You spoke your defects aloud. You admitted the patterns, the damage, the parts of yourself you'd rather not claim. Stillness, even mercy, greeted you instead of condemnation. As if The One listening already knew it all. And in that silence, the answer came.

"Let Him fix it."

So now, with nothing more than humility and trust, you ask.

You've done all the preparation. The writing. The sharing. The letting go. Now there's nothing left to polish or examine. This step is about humility. It's about saying to Allah: "I'm ready. Please remove what I can't."

When we ask Allah to remove our shortcomings, we're not chasing perfection—we're removing what's in the way. These defects don't just weigh us down emotionally. They distort our perception. They interrupt our relationship with the Divine. They slow our movement toward becoming who we truly are.

If Step Six was the silent stillness before the leap, Step Seven is the act of jumping. You don't leap with your body. You leap with your *heart*. It's the moment you look inward at the defects you finally become ready to release—and then ask The One who can actually remove them.

But when we surrender our pride and sincerely ask for help, that burden clears. The connection becomes smoother. The path becomes more visible. And the journey can continue—not because we fixed ourselves, but because we stopped trying to and turned to The One who can.

All because we asked.

Humbly.

Step 7: Humbly asked Him to remove our shortcomings.

Alcoholics Anonymous, (4th Edition):

- "We were now at Step Seven. Many of us said to our Maker, as we understood Him: 'My Creator, I am now willing that you should have all of me, good and bad.'" — p. 76

- "Humbly saying to ourselves many times each day 'Thy will be done.'" — p. 88

- "The chief activator of our defects has been self-centered fear—primarily fear that we would lose something we already possessed or would fail to get something we demanded." — p. 76

Twelve Steps and Twelve Traditions:

- "Indeed, the attainment of greater humility is the foundation principle of each of A.A.'s Twelve Steps. For without some degree of humility, no alcoholic can stay sober at all." — p. 70

- "The whole emphasis of Step Seven is on humility. It is really saying to us that we now ought to be willing to try humility in seeking the removal of our other shortcomings, just as we did when we admitted that we were powerless over alcohol, and came to believe that a Power greater than ourselves could restore us to sanity." — p. 76

Qur'anic References:

"But Allah has endeared to you the faith and has made it pleasing in your hearts, and has made hateful to you disbelief, defiance, and disobedience. Those are the [rightly] guided." (Qur'an, 49:7)

"Indeed, Allah loves those who constantly repent and loves those who purify themselves." (Qur'an, 2:222)

The Distinction Between Step Six and Seven

It's subtle but vital.

> Step Six said: "I am ready for these defects to be removed."
>
> Step Seven says: "I ask You, Allah, to remove them."
>
> Step Six was *internal* preparation.
>
> Step Seven is *external* supplication.
>
> Step Six acknowledged our powerlessness over our defects.
>
> Step Seven acknowledges Allah's power to transform them.

These distinctions are crucial because many people get stuck between these steps. They become ready, but never actually ask. They recognize the problem but never surrender it. They prepare the ground, but never plant the seed.

This step is the first time in the process where we name Allah as *Al-Quddūs*, the Most Pure. We invoke His Purity to cleanse our hearts.

In the language of Islam, this step is *tawba*, repentance. But not just regret—return. Returning to the One who knows your heart, who allowed you to see your defects, and who alone can remove them.

And it's also *Tazkiyah*—the process of purifying the soul. This isn't about self-improvement. It's about Divine refinement. As the Qur'an says:

> *"But Allah has endeared to you the faith and has made it pleasing in your hearts, and has made hateful to you disbelief, defiance, and disobedience. Those are the rightly guided."*
>
> Qur'an, 49:7

This Step Seven moves us toward not forced compliance, but inner transformation. Loving the light and hating the darkness—not out of fear, but because the soul has awakened.

Metaphorical Quality Control

The title "Quality Control" may seem strange for a step about humility and surrender. In industry, quality control isn't about the manufacturer's ego; it's about ensuring the product meets the standards required for its purpose.

Similarly, in Step Seven, we're not trying to become perfect by our own definition. We're asking Allah to align us with His standards, to make our hearts suitable for the journey He has decreed for us. We surrender to Divine quality control, trusting that Allah knows better than we do what needs to be removed and what needs to remain.

Foundational Humility

The 12 & 12 says it plainly: humility is the foundation of all spiritual progress. That's because pride is the veil that keeps us clinging to our defects.

We hold on to things we secretly believe serve us. That biting sarcasm? It's just wit. That control obsession? It's just leadership. That passive-aggression? Oh, we call it boundaries. The *nafs* is clever like that. It disguises disease as identity.

When we become truly humble, when we drop the defenses and stand before Allah bare-hearted, we see the truth. Our character defects aren't quirks. They're chains. And humility is the key.

> *"Whoever humbles himself for the sake of Allah, Allah will raise him."*
> Prophet Muhammad (SAW), Sahih Muslim 2588

Step Seven is the moment we bow.

Not because we are worthless. But because we are finally beginning to see our worth—and we want to be clean.

The Illusion of Fixing Yourself

Step Seven breaks one of the deepest lies the ego tells: that we can fix ourselves. It is a revisit to the First Step when we realized our powerlessness over alcohol. In a similar vein, we are powerless over our character defects.

You can't. You never could. That's how you ended up here.

We don't work the steps to become our own gods—we work them to stop pretending that we were ever in control. We declare our imperfections to be offerings, not failures: "Ya Allah, this part of me is broken." I see that now. I've tried to fix it, justify it, ignore it—and I've failed. I give it to You."

Because the genuine humility of this step is not just in asking—it's in admitting that only Allah can purify what the ego has corrupted.

> *"And do not claim yourselves to be pure. He is most knowing of who fears Him."*
>
> Qur'an, 53:32

This verse should stop us cold.

Even now—at this point in the journey—there's still a part of us that wants to say, "I've come so far. I've done the work. Look at me." But the moment you claim purity is the moment you step out of *tawhid* and back into self-worship.

That's the danger of spiritual pride: the belief that transformation is your accomplishment, not His Mercy.

Step Seven reminds us: **You are not your own savior.**

Sujood and the Anatomy of Humility

In Islam, humility is more than just a feeling. It's an act.

During each prayer, we prostrate. We put our foreheads to the ground. The most honored part of our body lowered to the floor.

And in that position, something subtle and sacred happens.

The heart is elevated above the head.

The head, home of the *nafs*, the ego, the voice of control, is silenced. The heart, seat of sincerity and Divine presence, is lifted.

We do this 34 times a day in the five obligatory prayers. And if you linger in *sujood*—if you whisper your *du'a* with a humble heart—you'll find something else:

You are not alone down there. You are seen.

> "And We have already created man and know what his soul whispers to him, and We are nearer to him than [his] jugular vein."

Qur'an, 50:16

We feel Him most reverently with our heads lowered and our hearts elevated.

In Step Seven, we supplicate Allah to remove our defects of character. But what makes that asking powerful is the awareness that we are not calling upon a distant God, but One who is already closer than we realize.

- We don't need ornate language or perfect words. Allah already knows what we're struggling to say.

- Our sincerity is heard before it's spoken. The humility of Step Seven is already visible to Him before we ever put it into words.

- True transformation begins by recognizing His nearness. We are not begging for His attention—we're simply turning toward what was always near.

"He who opens the door of humility, Allah will open for him the door of mercy."

Ibn Qayyim al-Jawziyya, Madarij al-Salikin

The Path of Purification: *Tazkiyah*

"We needed new habits of activity to fill those open spaces and utilize the nervous energy previously absorbed by our preoccupation, or our obsession, with drinking."

Living Sober, p. 28

This insight mirrors the Islamic concept of *tazkiyah*, the purification and cultivation of the soul. In Islam, purification isn't just about removing harmful traits; it's about replacing them with life-giving ones. As we release old behaviors that once defined our addiction, we must also plant new ones: habits of *dhikr*, prayer, service, and reflection. These direct the heart to grow in alignment with divine purpose. *Tazkiyah* is active. It's a process of transformation that fills the spiritual vacuum with presence and intention. Step Seven, like *tazkiyah*, is about renewal.

When we ask Allah to remove our defects in Step Seven, we are asking Him to clear the path for that flourishing. It's a prayer for inner expansion: for clarity, sincerity, and humility. Allowing the free alignment of the heart with the Creator.

> *"He has succeeded who purifies it, and he has failed who instills it with corruption."*
>
> Qur'an, 91:9-10

This is no metaphor. It's the final scorecard.

Everything we do, prayer, fasting, charity, even recovery, brings the heart into a state of purity. A heart free from arrogance, jealousy, manipulation, fear, greed, and self-delusion. A heart fit to stand before Allah.

Step Seven is where we stop polishing the outside and ask Allah to clean the inside.

Because of these defects we've listed? They're not just annoyances. They're not bad habits. They are the grime that blocks the light of faith. They are the rust on the mirror of the soul.

And here's the secret: we don't get purified by force. We get purified by consent.

> *"Allah will not change the condition of a people until they change what is in themselves."*
>
> Qur'an, 13:11

This is spiritual consent. Saying, "Yes, Ya Rabb. I see what's in me. I want it out. I trust You to remove it."

It is the truest kind of *du'a*. The prayer of someone who has stopped pretending, stopped negotiating, and started surrendering.

Divine Contradiction

This is one of the strangest truths of recovery, and one of the most beautiful secrets in the *deen*: you become strong the moment you admit you're weak.

Everything in the *dunya* tells us to be self-made. To push harder. Hustle. Grind. Show no weakness. But Step Seven whispers a different truth:

"You can't fix yourself. But you can be fixed."

And in Islam, this truth is everywhere.

The Qur'an never tells us to become powerful on our own. It tells us to seek refuge. To submit. To humble ourselves. And in return, Allah grants us what no effort alone could achieve: protection, guidance, elevation, and strength.

> *"Indeed, Allah is with those who fear Him and those who are doers of good."*
>
> Qur'an, 16:128

When we take Step Seven, we're not just asking for a better personality. We're asking to become someone who walks upright again. Someone whose heart is clean enough to carry light.

But to get there, we have to give up the illusion that we're strong enough to heal ourselves.

Therefore, the *nafs* resists Step Seven more than any other. Because the *nafs* doesn't want to surrender. It wants to achieve. It wants to say, "Look what I did. Look how spiritual I've become." And that is the very poison we're trying to have removed.

Let's be clear: you will not be the one who removes your defects.

> *"...And it is He who accepts repentance from His servants and pardons misdeeds, and He knows what you do."*
>
> Qur'an, 42:25

The humility of Step Seven is knowing where the power lies—and asking sincerely for that power to purify your heart.

Suggested Du'a

"O Allah, grant my soul its taqwā and purify it. You are the best of those who purify. You are its Guardian and Protector."

Prophet Muhammad (SAW), Sahih Muslim 2722

This prophetic *du'ā*, made in humility and sincerity, mirrors the essence of Step Seven: recognizing our dependence on God to remove our defects and purify our character. Both traditions emphasize surrender, purification, and service.

"My Lord, I am now willing that You should have all of me—my strengths and my flaws. Remove from me everything that stands in the way of my service to You. Use me as You will. Āmīn."
Adapted from the Seventh Step Prayer, Alcoholics Anonymous, p. 76

This adaptation of the Seventh Step Prayer preserves its spirit while placing it in the devotional language of Islamic prayer. Like the du'a of the Prophet ﷺ it centers the act of *tawbah*—turning back to Allah, with a sincere desire for purification and service.

Reflection Questions—Step Seven

1. What does humility mean to me, and how does it shape the way I ask Allah for help?

2. Do I truly believe that Allah can remove my shortcomings—or do I still rely on my strength to change?

3. How can I practice surrender daily without falling into passivity or self-pity?

Enjoying a Wholesome Heart

As we complete Step Seven, we are lighter. The burdens we've carried—those ingrained character defects—have loosened their grip. Not by our strength, but through Divine Mercy, we humbly ask for.

When we supplicate Allah to remove our defects, we're not summoning Him from afar—we're speaking to The One who says, "*We are nearer to him than his jugular vein.*" (Qur'an, 50:16) That nearness makes real surrender possible. He already knows. He's already there. And He's waiting for us to ask.

This is not the end of our transformation. Defects may reappear in new disguises. Old habits may try to reassert themselves. But now we possess the most powerful tool in recovery: the honest admission that we cannot purify ourselves, paired with the deep trust that Allah responds to sincere requests for change.

Step Seven marks a transition from the inward clearing of the first six steps to the outward living that follows. With a heart more attuned to the Divine will, we now turn toward making amends, practicing these principles in our daily lives, and offering hope to others.

"Verily Allah raises those who humble themselves for His sake."—The Prophet Muhammad (SAW), *Sahih Muslim* 2588.

Having humbled ourselves, we are now ready to be lifted by the Mercy of Allah. And from that place of Divine uplift, we can see the road ahead with greater clarity.

Humility is a way of moving through the *dunya*. It's a posture of the soul. One we return to again and again, each time saying: "Ya Allah, I still need Your help. I'm not finished. Keep removing what stands between me and Your light."

And with each sincere prayer, the heart grows a little clearer, the path a little straighter, and our journey a little more aligned with *qadr*—the Divine story written for us before we were even born.

Chapter Eight

Stained Ledger

I t's time to set our sights outward. For a time, we paused, anchored in deep introspection, surrender, and spiritual housecleaning. Step Four helped us map out the truth of our past. Step Five brought that truth into the open. Steps Six and Seven invite us to release the parts of ourselves that can not continue on this journey.

Now, with clearer hearts and fewer burdens, we're ready to face outward again.

We venture forth with purpose. Step Eight gives us a sense of direction. A clear path toward healing what we've broken.

Step Eight calls us to "make a list of all persons we had harmed and become willing to make amends to them all." This step prepares the heart for the amends that follow in Step Nine. This is about clarity and willingness. It's about facing the truth of what we've done and preparing our hearts to make it right.

We begin with what we already know. Here is where we revisit our inventory from Step Four. We have a nice, long list of resentments toward people who more often than not, we owe amends. Wherever there is resentment, there's often unresolved harm or guilt. So we return to those names, and we ask:

What was my part? What harm did I cause?

Then, we widen the lens. We add names that weren't in those inventories. People we hurt through silence, neglect, dishonesty, or selfishness. The list evolves as our awareness deepens. It may grow. That's okay. We start by opening our hearts to reconciliation.

Because a heart that will make things right is a heart that's ready to draw near to Allah. Our willingness to take responsibility, to repair, and restore is, itself, a form of worship.

Step 8: Made a list of all persons we had harmed, and became willing to make amends to them all.

Alcoholics Anonymous (4th Edition):

- "We attempt to sweep away the debris which has accumulated out of our effort to live on self-will and run the show ourselves. If we haven't the will to do this, we ask until it comes."— p. 76

- "Now we go out to our fellows and repair the damage done in the past..."— p. 76

- "We made it when we took inventory. We subjected ourselves to a drastic self-appraisal."— p. 76

- "If we haven't the will to do this, we ask until it comes. Remember it was agreed at the beginning we would go to any lengths for victory over alcohol."— p. 76

Twelve Steps and Twelve Traditions:

- "Every A.A. has found that he can make little headway... until he first backtracks and really makes an accurate and unsparing survey of the human wreckage he has left in his wake."— p. 77

- "The readiness to take the full consequences of our past acts... is the very spirit of Step Eight."— p. 79

- "It is the beginning of the end of isolation from our fellows and from God."— p. 77

Qur'anic Reference:

"And establish weight in justice and do not make deficient the balance." (Qur'an, 55:9)

Revisiting the Inventory

In many ways, Step Eight is a refined reworking of Step Four.

Where Step Four exposed the inner damage, Step Eight moves to the external.

We already made a list back in Step Four. The inventory of our resentments, fears, and sexual conduct. A moral ledger. A map of where our ego, our wounds, and our impulses collided with the lives of others.

While Step Four was about writing it out, Step Eight is about spiritual responsibility. It is the moment we ask: What harm did my pain cause others? What damage did my character defects leave in their wake?

This is where the insight from Steps Six and Seven serves a new purpose.

Identifying our defects doesn't mean we're done with them. Learning about them isn't the same as removing them. Even asking Allah to take them away doesn't mean they're gone.

Sometimes, Allah in His mercy allows those very defects to linger as signposts.

Pride might still appear, but now we can see how it has shaped our past behavior. Control might still creep in, but now we can recognize the wreckage it leaves behind.

Each lingering defect can act like a compass needle, pointing us toward the people we need to make things right with.

If Step Four was the excavation, Step Eight is the blueprint for reconstruction.

Revisiting *Adab* in Recovery

In addiction, our *adab* deteriorated severely. We may have maintained a facade of courtesy or religiosity, but our true conduct, especially in private, often violated the principles we claimed to value. We were harsh when we should have been gentle. We were deceptive when we should have been truthful. We were absent when we should have been present.

Step Eight calls us to repair this damage; not only through honesty, but through the restoration of proper *adab* in our relationships. This step is more than just a list; it is a spiritual preparation to face others with humility, accountability, and care. And one of the most powerful forms that *adab* can take in this context is *ithar*.

Ithar means giving preference to others over oneself. It is the generosity that extends beyond material giving. It reflects a heart that will be uncomfortable for the sake of someone else's dignity or healing.

> "*Ithar* is one of the highest ranks of generosity, and the perfection of good character. It is to give preference to others over oneself in matters of religion and the world."
>
> Ibn Qayyim al-Jawziyya, Madarij al-Salikin

In our active addiction, we did the opposite. We placed our comfort, our avoidance, and our self-interest above the harm we were causing. Now, through this step, we reverse that pattern. When we say, "Your dignity matters. Your healing matters. The harm I caused you matters," we are practicing *ithar*. In doing so, we are restoring the spiritual dimension of *adab*.

Making amends isn't just a moral obligation; it is an act of sacred generosity. When done with *ithar*, it becomes a sign that our transformation is not just internal but visible in how we walk back into the world.

Step Symbiosis

Like Steps Six and Seven, which work together as inner readiness followed by surrender, Steps Eight and Nine form a similar pairing; preparation and action. Step Six was about becoming entirely ready; Step Seven was about humbly asking. Step Eight now calls us to become willing to make amends; Step Nine is where that willingness becomes real. One step clears the heart; the next calls Divine power into action. The internal must precede the external, expressing the natural rhythm of real transformation.

In Step Eight, we create the list and develop willingness. In Step Nine, we actually make the amends. This distinction is crucial. Many people rush into making amends before they've thoroughly prepared their list or developed true willingness. Step Eight gives us time to ensure we're approaching amends from a place of spiritual readiness rather than impulsivity or avoidance.

So we return to the Fourth Step list with fresh eyes.

We revisit our conduct through the lens of the defects we named in Step Six, and the humility we cultivated in Step Seven.

We are searching carefully for the next layer of our healing.

Our job in Step Eight is to plan what we need to fix.

Practical Guidance:

Making a thorough Step Eight list requires both courage and method. Here are some practical approaches:

1. Start with your Fourth Step inventory: Look at the "My Part" column from your resentment inventory. Each place you identified your role in a situation likely points to someone you harmed.

2. Categories of harm: Consider different harms to ensure thoroughness.

   ○ Financial harm: People you stole from, didn't repay, or financially exploited

   ○ Emotional harm: Those you betrayed, manipulated, or abused emotionally

   ○ Physical harm: Anyone you have threatened or physically hurt

   ○ Spiritual harm: Those whose faith or values you undermined or mocked

   ○ Relational harm: Friends and family you neglected or abandoned

3. The difficult additions: Force yourself to include:

   ○ People you're still angry at

   ○ People who also harmed you

   ○ Institutions and groups, not just individuals

   ○ Yourself (many of us need to make amends to ourselves)

4. For each name, identify the specific harm. Be concise but thorough. "I lied about where the money went." "I abandoned our friendship when they needed me." "I spread rumors about them."

5. Separate list-making from willingness: You can put someone on your list even if you don't yet feel willing to make amends. Prayer and reflection can develop

willingness.

6. Keep the list private but accessible: This document contains sensitive information about others. Treat it with appropriate confidentiality.

Remember: this list is a living document. As you progress in recovery, new names may surface. That's a sign of growth. Add them as they come to mind.

Islamic Principles for Creating Your List

Islamic tradition offers several principles that can guide us in creating a thorough and sincere Step Eight list:

> *"Allah loves that when one of you performs a deed, he does it with excellence."*
>
> Prophet Muhammad (SAW), Shu'ab al-'Īmān by al-Bayhaqī, Hadith 5311

1. Thoroughness (*itqan*): Approaching your inventory with this spirit of excellence means being thorough, honest, and unwilling to take shortcuts or make excuses.

2. Justice (*'adl*): The Qur'an repeatedly emphasizes justice, even against ourselves: *"O you who believe, be persistently standing firm in justice, witnesses for Allah, even if it be against yourselves..."* (Qur'an, 4:135). This means including everyone we harmed, not just those it's comfortable to face.

3. Truth (*sidq*): As Muslims, we are directed to always be truthful, whether that truth favors us or harms us. Truthfulness is essential in identifying the actual harm we caused, not minimizing or justifying it. The Qur'an states: *"O you who believe, fear Allah and be with those who are truthful"* (Qur'an, 9:119).

4. Mercy (*rahmah*): While we must be honest about harm, we should approach our list with mercy toward ourselves. Avoid using it as an opportunity for self-flagellation. Remember, this is about healing.

5. Sacred privacy (*sitr*): In Islam, concealing sins is valued when it doesn't infringe on others' rights. You should keep your Step Eight list confidential. Shared sparingly and only with your sponsor or spiritual advisor. Discernment is vital.

These principles help ensure that our list is not just a mechanical exercise, but a sacred act of accountability aligned with our spiritual values.

> *"And those who, when they commit an immorality or wrong themselves [by transgression], remember Allah and seek forgiveness for their sins—and who can forgive sins except Allah?—and [who] do not persist in what they have done while they know."*
>
> Qur'an, 3:135

This verse affirms the sincerity of self-accountability as a path to forgiveness. It describes a heart that sees its wrongs and turns. Exactly what Step Eight calls for. It reminds us that even in moments of failure; it is the return that matters most.

> *"Whoever has wronged another concerning his reputation or anything else should beg him to forgive him before the Day of Resurrection, when there will be no money to compensate for wrong deeds, but if he has good deeds, they will be taken from him according to the wrong he has done..."*
>
> Prophet Muhammad (SAW), Sahih al-Bukhari, 6534

This hadith is directly relevant to Step Eight. It reminds us that we cannot afford to carry these debts into the next life. If we know we've wronged someone, the time to make it right is now, while we still can.

Practical Accountability

Who did we hurt?

This isn't about what happened to us. It's about what we did. The selfishness. The dishonesty. The carelessness. The trust we shattered.

It is important that we avoid shame and focus on clarity. Because if we don't see the harm we've done, we can't heal it. We can't make it right. We certainly can't stop ourselves from repeating it.

> "We need to examine, carefully and honestly, just what harm we have done others... We're looking for our mistakes."
>
> Twelve Steps and Twelve Traditions, p. 52

It's tempting to justify or compare: "Yeah, but they..."

That's not the point. The point is:

Where did I cause pain? Where did I act out of ego, fear, or self-preservation?

Sometimes it's obvious: we cheated, stole, lied.

Sometimes it's subtle: we ghosted, manipulated, withheld love, or stayed silent when we should've spoken.

Every act of harm matters, even the quiet ones.

Willingness is a Spirit Pivot

The phrase "become willing" in Step Eight might seem passive, but it represents one of the most profound spiritual practices in recovery. Willingness is a quality we cultivate through consistent spiritual effort.

In Islamic spirituality, this cultivation of willingness aligns with the concepts of *rida* (contentment with Divine decree) and *taslim* (submission). It requires us to surrender our ego's resistance and align our will with Allah's will.

When we find ourselves unwilling to make amends to someone on our list, we are essentially saying: "I know what Allah requires, but I'm not ready to follow it." This resistance is natural; it's human. Recognize that it is also a spiritual obstacle that Step Eight invites us to address.

> *"Make things easy and do not make them difficult. Give glad tidings and do not drive people away."*
>
> Prophet Muhammad (SAW, Sahih al-Bukhari, Hadith 6125

Sometimes, becoming willing starts with the simple acknowledgment: "I'm not willing yet, but I'm willing to become willing."

Here are spiritual practices that can help cultivate willingness:

- *Du'a* for softening the heart: "O Allah, remove the hardness from my heart toward this person."

- Reflecting on your own need for forgiveness: "Just as I hope Allah forgives me, let me become willing to seek forgiveness from others."

- *Salat al-Istikhara*: Praying for guidance specifically about your willingness to make amends.

- *Dhikr* focused on Allah's names of mercy: Reciting *Al-Rahman* and *Al-Raheem* to remind yourself of Divine compassion.

- Visualizing the interaction with a positive outcome: Imagine how sincere amends will lift the burden.

Remember: willingness doesn't mean you're no longer afraid. It means you're ready to act despite the fear, trusting that the path of accountability is the path to freedom.

Divine Accountability

"And establish weight in justice and do not make deficient the balance."

Qur'an, 55:9

Don't imbalance the world with your ego. Don't violate the trust (*amanah*) that others placed in you. This is *muhasaba*, reckoning. A willingness to face the full impact of our lives without excuses.

"Do you know who the bankrupt person is?" "The one who comes on the Day of Judgment with prayer, fasting, and zakah, but also having insulted this one, falsely accused that one, devoured the wealth of another, shed blood, and beaten others. His good deeds will be distributed to those he wronged. If they run out, their sins will be cast upon him..."

Prophet Muhammad (SAW). Sahih Muslim 2581

Spiritual success isn't only about prayer. It's about justice.

And if it still lives in us, it belongs here.

- Where was I selfish, dishonest, inconsiderate, or manipulative?

- Where did I harm others out of my own unhealed pain?

- Where did I violate trust, even in small ways?

- Where have I never truly taken responsibility?

Kindness, Clarity, and the Whisper of the *Nafs*

Step Eight is a spiritual checkpoint.

We are called to face the wreckage of our past with honesty and courage. We approach it with sincerity, grounded in the desire to heal and grow.

The *nafs* is cunning. It may try to downplay our actions: "They deserved it." Or it may drag us into despair: "You're broken. You'll never fix this."

Both are lies.

Don't overthink this. Remember, we are cultivating willingness. To become better. To make things right. To take responsibility not only for what we did, but to pave the way for who we're becoming.

This list isn't just a record of harm. It's a mirror to our defects. Unchecked fear, arrogance, dishonesty, and selfishness produced these results.

But we are no longer that person. That was the self in rebellion. This is the self in surrender

We include everyone we harmed. Not just the easy ones. Not just the ones we think will forgive us. Step Eight says all. That means some very difficult, humbling, even humiliating conversations may lie ahead.

The *nafs* resists this. It hates to admit fault. It hates to ask for forgiveness.

Remember, our path is not about feeding the ego. We are freeing our hearts.

Reflection Questions – Step Eight

1. What patterns do I notice in the harm I caused, and what do they reveal about the fears or character defects that were influencing my behavior?

2. Where is my willingness to make amends still limited by pride, fear, or the desire to protect myself?

3. How can I approach each person on my list with sincere concern for their dignity and healing, even if it means stepping outside my comfort zone?

Willing to Action

The process of making this list and becoming willing to make amends represents a pivotal transition in our journey. The names we've written are more than just people. These names mark our responsibility, remind us where we caused harm, and invite us to repair what we can. We are now moving from inward transformation to outward action. Step Eight prepares us for the direct, often uncomfortable work of Step Nine: the act of making amends. It will require courage, humility, and spiritual clarity.

Some conversations ahead may be painful. Some may unfold more gently than we expect. But each amend is a step toward integrity. A return to alignment with truth, with justice, and with the person we are becoming in recovery.

> *"O you who believe, be persistently standing firm in justice..."*
>
> Qur'an, 4:135

This is the heart of Step Eight is sincerity. The willingness to stand in front of our past, acknowledge our wrongs without excuse, and prepare to make them right without condition.

The list is complete for now, though we may add to it as our self-awareness grows. For some names, full willingness may still develop, and that's okay. Willingness is a process, not a performance. The point is, we have named the things we must face. We've turned our attention from contemplation to accountability.

The path ahead will stretch us, but we are no longer walking it alone. We move forward, guided by honest intention, carried by Divine mercy, and grounded in the truth that real freedom only comes when we stop running.

Chapter Nine

You Owe

The way forward is clear now. Step Eight gave us the list. Line by line, we named the people we had harmed. We faced the damage honestly: broken trust, fractured relationships, missed obligations. That list became our guide.

Now, Step Nine turns intention into action.

This is where we repair. One conversation at a time. One person at a time. We reach out to those we've hurt: family, friends, former partners, employers. Some welcome us with open hearts. Some still carry the weight of our actions. Others want nothing to do with us, and we honor that, too.

We move forward with discernment.

We don't demand forgiveness. We don't fix everything in one moment. We show up with humility, with truth, and with a willingness to take responsibility.

Making amends straightforwardly involves repaying what is owed, speaking the truth, and asking how to make things right. Other amends present complicated, unclear, or impossible situations. In those cases, we make living amends. By changing how we show up in the world. We serve. We give. We grow. We let our changed behavior speak where our words are no longer welcome.

This isn't about relieving guilt. It's about clearing the space between us and Allah.

Because we cannot move forward with integrity until we have faced our past with humility.

Step Nine isn't dramatic. It isn't a performance. It's one honest amend after another, kept grounded in sincerity, guided by principle.

We move forward, not to run away from our past, but to celebrate the chance to transform into our destined selves.

Step 9: Made direct amends to such people wherever possible, except when to do so would injure them or others.

Big Book of Alcoholics Anonymous (4th Edition):

- "We go to them in a helpful and forgiving spirit, confessing our former ill feeling and expressing our regret." (p. 77)

- "Our real purpose is to fit ourselves to be of maximum service to God and the people about us." (p. 77)

- "We must not shrink at anything. We are there to sweep off our side of the street..." (p. 77)

- "If we are painstaking about this phase of our development, we will be amazed before we are halfway through." (p. 83)

Twelve Steps and Twelve Traditions:

- "Step Nine restores in us a clear conscience and new peace of mind." (p. 83)

- "We should be sensible, tactful, considerate and humble without being servile or scraping." (p. 83)

- "It should not be done impulsively or unnecessarily." (p. 83)

- "Good judgment, a careful sense of timing, courage and prudence—these are the qualities we shall need when we take Step Nine." (p. 83)

Qur'anic Reference:

"Indeed, Allah commands you to render trusts to whom they are due and when you judge between people to judge with justice. Excellent is that which Allah instructs you. Indeed, Allah is ever Hearing and Seeing." (Qur'an, 4:58)

The Four Types of Amends

Step Nine involves different approaches to amends, each appropriate for different situations.

1. Direct Amends

These are face-to-face conversations where we acknowledge specific harms, take responsibility without excuse, and ask how we might make things right. Direct amends are appropriate when:

- The person is accessible

- Meeting won't cause additional harm

- We can take responsibility, expecting nothing in return

Example: "I stole money from you when I was using. I was wrong, and I want to repay you. I can offer $100 now and $100 each month until it's paid back."

2. Indirect Amends

When direct contact isn't possible or would cause harm, we find alternative ways to make repair:

- Composing letters that might never get sent

- Donating to causes that matter to the person

- We will make a general form of restitution that honors what was taken

Example: For a deceased relative we harmed, we might support their favorite charity or help their children.

3. Living Amends

These are the ongoing changes in behavior that show our commitment to being different.

- Becoming reliable when we were unreliable

- Being present when we were absent

- Being honest when we were deceptive

Example: A father who neglected his children makes a living amends by consistently showing up for them now; attending events, keeping promises, being emotionally available.

4. Amends to Ourselves

We often neglect the harm we cause ourselves through addiction.

- Self-neglect

- Abandoning our dreams and values

- Self-hatred and punishment

Example: Committing to self-care, education, or developing talents we abandoned during active addiction.

In all cases, Islamic principles guide us: *ikhlas* (sincerity), *ihsan* (excellence), and *adl* (justice) must be present. We don't make amends to check a box; we make them to restore harmony and honor Allah's command to render trusts to whom they are due.

Beyond "I'm Sorry"

In active addiction, many of us became experts at empty apologies. "I'm sorry" became a phrase we used to escape consequences rather than to accept them. Therefore Step Nine doesn't use the word "apologize". The step clearly says "amends."

The difference is profound.

Apologies are about *words*.

- They focus on feelings

- They can be quick and easy

- They often center on the apologizer's emotions

- They require only momentary discomfort

Amends are about *restoration*.

- They focus on actions

- They take time and sustained effort

- They center on the harm that was caused

- They require an ongoing commitment to change

In Islamic terms, this is the difference between lip service and true *tawbah* (repentance). The Qur'an warns:

> *"O you who have believed, why do you say what you do not do? Great is*
> *hatred in the sight of Allah that you say what you do not do."*
>
> Qur'an, 61:2-3

True amends align our actions with our words. We don't just say we're different. We show it consistently.

When we told our families "I'm sorry" for the hundredth time, they didn't need more words; they needed change. They needed reliability, honesty, presence, and integrity.

That's why the most powerful amends often begin with listening rather than speaking. Instead of launching into our prepared speech, we might simply ask: "How did my behavior affect you?" and then truly hear the answer.

Amends repair. Apologies explain. And in recovery, repair matters more than explanation.

People will easily forgive you for being wrong. They will not forgive you for being right. Now, turn that around. Step Nine teaches us that many amends will require not only humility, but the courage to admit that others were right about us. This means having the conversations we really don't want to have.

Most of these almost always are with the people who are closest to us. The people whose trust you broke, the ones you lied to, used, and betrayed. These are the people who may never want to see you again, and that is their right.

Here is where **discernment** becomes crucial.

The phrase "except when to do so would injure them or others" is crucial guidance in Step Nine. It requires spiritual discernment and honest consultation with sponsors, mentors, or spiritual advisors.

Situations where direct amends might cause more harm include:

1. When it would reveal harmful information - If your amend would expose secrets that would hurt innocent parties, such as admitting to stealing money from a family business in a way that implicates or damages another relative who was unaware, it may do more harm than good. In such cases, spiritual guidance and discernment are essential to ensure the amend doesn't create new wounds in the process of healing old ones.

2. When it would trigger trauma - If approaching someone would reopen wounds they've worked hard to heal

3. When it would violate boundaries - If the person has explicitly asked you to stay away

4. When it would create legal jeopardy - For serious crimes where legal consequences are appropriate

5. When it would appear manipulative - If your timing seems calculated to gain advantage

In these cases, indirect or living amends become the appropriate path. This isn't avoidance, this is wisdom.

The Islamic principle of harm reduction applies here.

> *"There should be neither harm nor reciprocating harm."*
> The Prophet Muhammad (SAW) Sunan Ibn Majah, no. 2340

Making an amend that causes new harm contradicts this principle.

Remember: The goal is healing, not self-relief. Sometimes the most sincere amends is giving someone the space they need, changing our behavior, and making restitution in ways that don't require their participation.

This requires humility. We acknowledge that our desire to make amends doesn't override others' right to protection from further harm.

The Anatomy of an Amend

Making effective amends requires preparation, presence, and practice. Here's a framework that honors both recovery principles and Islamic *adab* (spiritual etiquette):

Preparation

1. Pray first - Seek Allah's guidance and purify your intention

2. Consult your sponsor - Discuss your plan and check your motives

3. Be specific - Know exactly what harm you're addressing

4. Plan restitution - If applicable, be ready to make concrete repair

5. Release expectations - Accept that you cannot control their response

The Conversation

1. Express gratitude - Thank them for meeting with you

2. State your purpose - "I'm in recovery and making amends for past harms"

3. Name the specific harm - "I lied to you about..." or "I failed to..."

4. Take full responsibility - No "but" statements, no shifting blame

5. Offer repair - "How can I make this right?" or offer specific restitution

6. Listen completely - Their feelings and perspective matter

7. Respect boundaries - Accept whatever response they give

What Not to Do

1. Don't expect or ask for forgiveness - That's their choice to give or withhold

2. Don't make excuses - "I was using" is context, not justification

3. Don't interrupt their response - Even if it's painful to hear

4. Don't defend yourself - This isn't a debate

5. Don't make it about your pain - Your guilt is not their burden

Islamic Perspective

The Prophet Muhammad (SAW) demonstrated reconciliation through:

- Humility without self-degradation

- Truth without harshness

- Responsibility without excuses

- Generosity without expectation

Remember the hadith: *"He who has in his heart the weight of a mustard seed of pride shall not enter Paradise."* Making amends is an exercise in removing pride and restoring harmony through sincere accountability.

Making Amends in the Digital Age

In today's interconnected world, some unique considerations arise when making amends:

1. Digital vs. In-Person - While face-to-face amends are preferred when possible, geographical distance or safety concerns may cause digital approaches. Video calls preserve some of the personal connection that text-based communication lacks.

2. Public vs. Private - Social media "apologies" are rarely appropriate amends. They often serve the apologizer more than the harmed party. True amends are typically private, person-to-person exchanges, not public performances.

3. Digital Permanence - Written digital communications (emails, messages) remain accessible indefinitely. Consider the implications of putting sensitive amends in writing.

4. Technological Boundaries - Being "blocked" on social media or other platforms is a boundary to be respected, not circumvented in the name of making amends.

5. Group Harms - If you harmed online communities or groups, consider how to make amends that respect the collective nature of the harm without creating further disruption.

The core principles remain the same: sincerity, responsibility, and respect for boundaries. Technology should serve these principles, not replace them.

Cultural Considerations

"The best of you are those who are best to their families, and I am the best among you to my family."

Prophet Muhammad (SAW), Tirmidhi 3895

Making amends within Muslim communities may involve additional cultural dynamics that require wisdom, sensitivity, and *adab* (etiquette). While the spiritual imperative to make amends remains unchanged, the how of that process may vary depending on cultural expectations, gender roles, and social structures. Below are some key considerations:

1. Family Honor (*'Izzah* or *Izzat*)—In many Muslim-majority cultures, there is a tradition. Making amends that reveal private wrongs, particularly those involving dishonor, can affect not only the individual but the extended family's standing in the community. In such cases, discretion and timing are essential. Consider making indirect amends, symbolic gestures, or living amends when direct disclosure may cause disproportionate harm or shame. Always weigh the impact on family reputation without using it as an excuse to avoid accountability.

2. Gender Dynamics—Islam emphasizes modesty and proper boundaries (*haya'*),

especially between unrelated men and women (*ghayr mahram*). In many traditional contexts, it may be inappropriate, or even unsafe, for a man and a woman to meet privately to make amends. A third party, such as a relative, elder, or trusted intermediary, can help facilitate the conversation respectfully. Alternatively, a written note, financial restitution, or an act of service may serve as culturally acceptable forms of amends that uphold Islamic etiquette.

3. Respect of Elders—Islam teaches deep reverence for elders, and this often translates into formal modes of speech, body language, and deference in tone. When making amends to older family members, teachers, or community leaders, respect must guide the delivery. That doesn't mean avoiding the truth, but expressing it with humility, gratitude, and careful language. Apologizing through action, such as consistent service or care, may be more meaningful than direct confrontation sometimes.

4. Community Involvement—In collectivist cultures, where one's actions affect the larger tribe, family, or neighborhood, community leaders (such as imams, elders, or respected family figures) may serve as mediators in the amends process. This is especially relevant when the harm caused has had public effects or involved multiple people. Seeking their guidance or blessing before initiating certain amends may also prevent misunderstandings or unintended escalation. This can lend spiritual weight and social acceptance to the act of reconciliation.

5. Restorative Justice (*Islah*)—Islamic teachings on islah (reform and reconciliation) offer a rich foundation for the spirit of amends. The Qur'an encourages mending broken things, forgiving when possible, and returning rights to those harmed. When formal amends are too dangerous or impractical, one can draw from Islamic models of reconciliation rooted in community healing, fairness, and dignity. This might involve charitable giving in someone's name, public restitution, or private spiritual offerings coupled with behavior change.

These considerations don't alter the necessity of Step Nine. They simply shape the form it may take. Making amends is not a one-size-fits-all process, especially in diverse Muslim communities with strong cultural frameworks. Seeking counsel from culturally informed sponsors, imams, or elders can help ensure that the spirit of the Step is preserved while honoring the social and spiritual integrity of all parties involved.

Discernment and Depth: Islamic Perspective

In Islam, amends aren't optional. They are part of *amanah,* our trust, our duty. When we harm someone, we don't just say *astaghfirullah* and walk away. We return what we took. We repair what we broke.

> *"Worship Allah and associate nothing with Him, and to parents do good, and to relatives, orphans, the needy..."*
>
> Qur'an, 4:36

You cannot neglect your family and expect to grow spiritually. That's not Islam. That's not recovery.

Addiction made us bow to our *nafs,* our lower selves. Step Nine helps us bow instead to what's right. To truth. To Allah.

But the ego is tricky. It will turn even our repentance into a performance. It will hunger for approval, disguised as virtue.

> *"Indeed, the soul is ever inclined to evil—except those upon whom my Lord has mercy."*
>
> Qur'an, 12:53

That's why *ikhlas* (sincerity) is critical. You might fool people. You might even fool your sponsor.

But you cannot fool Allah.

> *"Indeed, Allah knows what is within the breasts."*
>
> Qur'an, 67:13

Before making any amend, ask:

- Am I here to relieve guilt, or offer healing?

- Am I looking for closure, or for truth?

- Am I serving Allah, or my ego?

The answers to those questions will guide your next step.

Repair before Redemption

When I began my Step Nine journey, I approached it with both trepidation and eagerness. I wanted the relief of clearing my conscience, but I hadn't fully grasped that amends weren't about me feeling better, they were about **doing better**.

Some amends went smoothly. The easiest amends in my experience are the financial ones, simply pay what you owe. Others are more complicated, even painful. One person refused to see me at all, sending word through a mutual friend that they hated my guts. That was hard to accept, but not entirely surprising considering my earlier conduct. I had to respect their boundary and learn another lesson in humility.

Through it all, I learned that amends aren't always about obtaining forgiveness. They're more about offering repair. Some relationships were restored. Some weren't. But with each honest conversation, I felt something shift within me. I obtained a lightness, a clarity that had nothing to do with how the other person responded.

That's when I understood when my sponsor said, "We make amends for us, but not about us." The purpose wasn't my comfort or even my redemption. It was about honoring truth, restoring justice, and serving Allah by taking responsibility for the wake I'd left behind.

When Amends Are Rejected

Not every amend will be accepted. Some doors remain closed, and some wounds are too deep for a single conversation to heal. This reality can be painful, but it too contains spiritual lessons.

When someone refuses our amend, we must:

1. Honor their boundary - Their refusal is their right. Respecting it is part of our amend.

2. Examine our approach - Was our timing wrong? Was our manner appropriate? This isn't about blame but learning.

3. Continue our living amend - Changed behavior speaks louder than any words.

4. Release the outcome to Allah - We cannot force reconciliation. Only Allah changes hearts.

5. Maintain hope without expectation - Sometimes doors open years later when trust is rebuilt.

The Qur'an teaches us:

"Perhaps Allah will put, between you and those to whom you have been enemies among them, affection. And Allah is competent, and Allah is Forgiving and Merciful."

Qur'an, 60:7

This verse reminds us that reconciliation ultimately comes from Allah. Our job is sincere effort, not guaranteed results.

A refused amend doesn't mean a failed Step Nine. It means we're learning the hardest lesson of all: we cannot control others, only ourselves. Sometimes, the most profound amend is giving someone the space they need, even when it hurts us to do so.

Prayer and the Path of Surrender

We should not make every possible amend. Not because we're afraid—but because we've grown wise enough to know that showing up might cause more harm.

When you're uncertain... When your motives feel cloudy... When the door feels half -open...

Turn it over.

"...And consult them in affairs. Then when you have taken a decision, put your trust in Allah. Certainly, Allah loves those who rely upon Him."

Qur'an, 3:159

Some amends won't unfold the way we imagined.
But something else will.

A new door will open. A new person may cross your path. A new chance to walk the same principle with someone else.

Step Nine isn't just about what we do. It's about who we become.

The Fruits of Amends

The Big Book describes the transformative outcomes that appear through the process of making amends:

> "If we are painstaking about this phase of our development, we will be amazed before we are halfway through. We are going to know a new freedom and a new happiness. We will not regret the past nor wish to shut the door on it. We will comprehend the word serenity and we will know peace..."
>
> Alcoholics Anonymous p. 83-84

These aren't rewards for completing a task—they're the natural fruits of alignment with spiritual principles. In Islamic terms, this happens when we bring our actions into harmony with Divine guidance.

The transformation occurs in layers.

1. Freedom from shame - When we face our wrongs directly, they lose power over us

2. Restored integrity - Our inner and outer lives become aligned

3. Spiritual growth - We develop humility, courage, and compassion

4. Renewed relationships - Many (though not all) relationships find healing

5. Peace with the past - We no longer need to avoid or deny our history

These outcomes don't depend on how others receive our amends. They depend on our sincerity, thoroughness, and commitment to the process.

The Prophet Muhammad (SAW) said: *"The religion is sincerity."* When we make sincere amends, regardless of outcome, we align ourselves with this principle. We stop performing recovery and start living it.

And slowly, the weight we've carried, sometimes for decades, begins to lift. Not because we've escaped our past, but because we've finally faced it with honesty, courage, and faith.

Reflection Questions – Step Nine

- How can I approach each amends as an act of love and service, rooted in sincerity and spiritual growth?

- In what ways has making direct amends strengthened my trust in Allah and my commitment to change?

- What qualities do I want to carry into each conversation so that my presence reflects humility, courage, and compassion?

A Lighter Heart

As we complete the work of Step Nine, something inside us has shifted. The weight of unaddressed harm has lessened. The haze of avoidance has lifted. We're able to move forward with greater clarity and intention.

Some conversations brought warmth and reconciliation. Others brought silence or rejection. The process itself, and the willingness to face those we harmed and offer sincere repair, has transformed us in ways that go beyond outcomes.

Step Nine marks a profound transition in our recovery. The first eight steps centered on self-awareness and spiritual preparation. In Step Nine, we test those internal changes in the real world. Where principles become actions. Where private intention becomes public responsibility.

As we continue from here, we carry new tools for the road ahead.

- The ability to take responsibility without making excuses.

- The courage to confront painful truths without retreating.

- The humility to accept whatever response we receive.

- The commitment to live differently, and not just speak differently.

We never truly finish the work of making amends. As we grow in recovery, new awareness may reveal people we've overlooked. And our living amends; the quiet, daily effort to be honest, kind, and accountable becomes a lifelong path.

But now we walk forward, lighter, freer. The promise of the Big Book unfolds: "We will not regret the past nor wish to shut the door on it." Our past no longer defines us; it instructs us. The pain we caused becomes part of the wisdom we carry.

And as we step toward Step Ten, we prepare to integrate these principles of accountability into our daily lives. Step Ten will ask us to continue taking personal inventory and promptly admitting when we are wrong. Effectively making amends in real-time rather than after years of accumulation. The lessons of Step Nine become the foundation for this practice of ongoing spiritual maintenance.

With gratitude and courage, we move forward to face the truth, thankful for the mercy we received, especially for the mercy of Allah, who enabled us to start this journey of healing and return.

Chapter Ten

Preventative Maintenance

S tep Ten is our daily tool for spiritual upkeep. Just like a wise mechanic checks the engine before it fails, we examine ourselves regularly; not to punish or obsess, but to prevent small problems from turning into big ones. A little resentment today, if left unchecked, can become tomorrow's relapse. Continuous personal inventory is how we catch it early.

The first nine steps were a deep, thorough overhaul. Now we shift into routine care: the healthy habits that enrich our lives. We're no longer cleaning up the wreckage; instead, we're learning how to avoid new wreckage. With ongoing self-reflection, honest admission of fault, and prompt amends, we prevent the corrosion of our spiritual health.

This isn't about perfection. It's about awareness. When something feels off, an attitude, a reaction, a lingering bitterness, Step Ten gives us a way to address it immediately. We don't wait until our emotions spin out or we're overwhelmed by guilt and shame. We make small, daily adjustments that keep us in alignment with Allah's guidance.

Recovery is a process, not a place. It needs care and attention, like anything valuable. Step Ten is the daily check-in that keeps us honest, grounded, and growing. It reminds us that the goal isn't to avoid all mistakes, but to catch them early and respond with integrity before they take root.

Step 10: Continue to take personal inventory and when we were wrong, we promptly admitted it.

Big Book of Alcoholics Anonymous (4th Edition):

"Continued to take personal inventory and when we were wrong promptly admitted it."-p. 59

"This thought brings us to Step Ten, which suggests we continue to take personal inventory and continue to set right any new mistakes as we go along." -p. 84

"We are not cured of alcoholism. What we really have is a daily reprieve contingent on the maintenance of our spiritual condition." -p. 85

Twelve Steps and Twelve Traditions:

"Step Ten is a spiritual axiom: every time we are disturbed, no matter what the cause, there is something wrong with us." (p. 90)

"Our first objective will be the development of self-restraint." (p. 91)

Qur'anic Reference:

"O you who believe, be mindful of Allah, and let every soul look to what it has sent forth for tomorrow. And be mindful of Allah. Indeed, Allah is aware of all that you do." (Qur'an. 59:18)

Inventory with Gratitude

Remember that every one of us woke up this morning with untreated alcoholism. We are guaranteed nothing more than a daily reprieve, and even that is *directly contingent on the maintenance of our spiritual condition*. Maintenance means catching minor problems before they turn into enormous problems. It means catching thought-forms and negative intentions before they turn into amends. We monitor our decision-making. Are we making selfish, fear-based decisions or Allah-based decisions?

In Islam, we express this with *alhamdulillāh*, praise be to Allah. This is not just a phrase we say aloud, but a condition of the heart. It is gratitude for clarity, for the opportunity to take inventory, and for the awareness to examine ourselves honestly. We are thankful for the ability to recognize our faults and the willingness to grow. An attitude of gratitude helps mend the heart and shields us from the infection of unchecked character defects. It strengthens our *īmān* and keeps our recovery grounded. Gratitude is the foundation of lasting sobriety and a life that holds meaning.

> "The heart is like a mirror. If it is not polished regularly, it will be covered with rust and lose its clarity."
>
> Imam al-Ghazali, Ihya' 'Ulum al-Din, Book 21: "The Marvels of the Heart"

The Mercy of Allah has raised us from the pit, not because we earned it, but because we surrendered. Now that He has lifted us and granted us a new lease on life, we are called to walk with care, with gratitude, and with vigilance. A higher standard of conduct applies to us as Muslims, regardless of whether we are in recovery. For those of us who are, that standard becomes even more critical, because the implications of a slip are severe. Every one of us is only one drink away from insanity. It is vital to hold this perspective and remain aware of the seriousness of the disease.

We notice when our tone turns sharp. When our motives go murky. When our integrity slips, not in dramatic ways but in quiet ones. The *nafs* is sneaky, and drifting starts with subtlety.

And when we drift, and we will, we course-correct promptly. We are not trying to impress anyone. However, since we want to stay clean. We must stay aligned with the Mercy that saved us.

The Sacred Pause

The Sacred Pause is the single most important tool I use in sobriety. I turn to it whenever I face a situation that threatens either my sobriety or my serenity. These situations can be large or small, depending on the person and the moment. Triggers are different for everyone, but they share one essential quality: if left unchecked, they can escalate. And when they escalate, they become dangerous.

The key is to recognize the trigger as it arises and take the Sacred Pause. When I am spiritually aware and able to catch myself at the moment, I can pause, zoom out, take the long view, play the tape through, and realign my course of action.

The Sacred Pause is a direct manifestation of the Ninth Step promise: we will intuitively know how to handle situations that used to baffle us. The pause is the space where intuition lives. It begins with a breath. When we experience a triggering event, before we speak, before we act, before we do anything, we stop and breathe. That breath creates a small opening in which we can choose how to respond. It may be a split second, but it can shape everything that follows.

In that space, we will either react from a place of ego and anger or respond from a place of wisdom. What we choose depends on the condition of our heart. When we are spiritually grounded, we find the pause. That one moment can make the difference between respect and regret.

This is the real-life application of Step Ten, where we stop, breathe, and look clearly at what is unfolding. What is actually happening here? What am I feeling, and where is it coming from? If I act on this feeling, what are the likely consequences—not just now, but in the long term? Will this cause regret? Will it create unnecessary conflict, harm, or chaos?

> "Few of us are able to quickly realize that we ought to stop right then and there, and to turn inwardly to see just how much we ourselves are to blame."
>
> Twelve Steps and Twelve Traditions, pp. 90–91

The Sacred Pause gives us the time to recognize resentment before it becomes bitterness. It helps us notice a selfish motive before it turns into dishonesty. It protects us from doing or saying things we will later need to make amends for. Like many alcoholics, I hate making amends. Like many addicts, I can also be a brat when I do not get my way. I am far from perfect, and I can admit that some days the *dunya* and my *nafs* get the better of me. That is exactly why the Sacred Pause matters so much.

For me, part of taking the pause recognizes that my powerlessness extends beyond alcohol. It includes people, places, and things. I am not in control of the world around me. What I can control is my attitude, my outlook, and my perception. Perception is everything. Recognizing a trigger as it arises and choosing to meet it with *adab*, takes spiritual maturity. It requires a willingness to see the truth in the moment and respond from the heart.

This practice is not about walking on eggshells or falling into self-doubt. It is not spiritual anxiety. It is clarity. Grounded awareness helps us stay in alignment with our values, our program, and our faith. We only need one moment of clarity, and that one moment can change the course of the entire day.

To live in Step Ten is to use that pause intentionally. To maintain awareness in the present moment and to live, speak, and act from the heart.

Pausing in action

When we pause, we perform a spot-check inventory. This is most valuable in moments of emotional disturbance. Here are practical examples of how it works in daily life:

When Anger Arises

You feel a surge of anger when someone cuts you off in traffic. Instead of honking or cursing, you pause and ask:

- What am I really feeling? (Threatened, disrespected, powerless?)

- Is this worth disturbing my serenity?

- How would Allah have me respond to this situation?

This quick check often reveals that your anger is disproportionate to the situation, stemming from deeper issues or earlier triggers.

When Resentment Builds

A colleague receives praise for a project you contributed to significantly. You feel resentment building. Your spot-check might include:

- Why am I disturbed by this person's success?

- Am I seeking recognition rather than focusing on service?

- What fear underlies this resentment? (That I'm not valued? What fear causes this resentment? That I'm not valued? That others will overlook me?)

This awareness might lead you to congratulate your colleague sincerely rather than nurturing bitterness.

> "As we go through the day we pause, when agitated or doubtful, and ask for the right thought or action."
>
> Alcoholics Anonymous, p. 87

When Self-Pity Appears

You notice yourself thinking "poor me" thoughts when facing a challenge. Your inventory might look like:

- Am I focusing on what I lack rather than what I've been given?

- Would I trade my entire life for someone else's? (The answer is usually no.)

- How can I serve rather than seek comfort right now?

When Spiritual Pride Emerges

You judge others who aren't as "spiritually advanced" as you see yourself. Your spot-check includes:

- Am I using spirituality to feel superior?

- Have I forgotten how much mercy I've received?

- What might Allah be teaching me through this person?

The spot-check inventory doesn't require writing things down in these moments (though that can be helpful when possible). Often, it's simply a momentary realign your thoughts and intentions before proceeding.

The key is honesty without judgment. You're not condemning yourself. You're gathering accurate information to make better choices.

The Evolution of Awareness

Early recovery is often disorienting. It feels like a roller coaster; emotionally volatile, unpredictable, and overwhelming. Many of us spent years regulating our emotions with substances. When we remove those crutches, we're suddenly exposed to the raw intensity of life without the buffer. Existing can feel unfamiliar, even frightening.

The chaos doesn't end with detox or withdrawal. The emotional and mental turbulence often lingers far beyond the physical symptoms. In the beginning, the wreckage of our past is glaring. The harm we caused is undeniable. In those early inventories, the patterns are obvious, and the writing comes easily.

But as we grow, our awareness sharpens. What once seemed like minor issues now stand out more clearly. The work becomes more subtle, and so does the standard we hold ourselves to. The more responsibility we take on in life and in recovery, the more responsibility Allah will entrust us with. Ultimately, we are responsible for the state of our hearts and the way we conduct ourselves.

A harsh tone. A lingering judgment. A brief flash of arrogance. The moment we mentally check out of a conversation while pretending to listen. These are small indicators, but they matter. They signal misalignments that, if left unexamined, can quietly erode our spiritual condition.

Step Ten teaches us to notice these early. It's way more than just about avoiding relapse. It's about preserving clarity. Over time, sobriety matures into serenity. Abstinence deepens into self-awareness. The goal is no longer just to stay clean, but to stay clear.

We realize: recovery isn't just about not drinking or using. It's about living with presence, honesty, and peace of heart. What starts with sobriety ultimately leads to serenity. Step Ten helps us stay on that path.

The Art of Prompt Amends

Step Ten introduces an extra dimension to our amends process: promptness. Where Step Nine involves going back to address past harms, Step Ten calls us to address new mistakes as they happen. This real-time accountability requires both courage and finesse.

Why Promptness Matters

- It prevents the buildup of guilt and shame

- It keeps minor issues from becoming big ones

- It shows our commitment to change

- It offers immediate healing to those we've harmed

- It reinforces our spiritual progress

Guidelines for Effective Prompt Amends

1. Respond, don't react — Wait until you're calm enough to offer a sincere amends, but don't use "calming down" as an excuse for delay.

2. Be specific — Name exactly what you did: "I interrupted you repeatedly during the meeting" is better than "I was rude earlier."

3. Keep it simple — Avoid long explanations or justifications. "I spoke harshly to you. I was wrong, and I'm sorry" is often enough.

4. Focus on your behavior, not their reaction — "I raised my voice" rather than "I made you upset."

5. Offer repair when appropriate — "How can I make this right?" or a specific offer of restitution shows sincerity.

6. Accept consequences — If they're still upset or need time, respect that. Your

amend doesn't entitle you to forgiveness.

In Islamic Context

Making amends is not just a moral principle in recovery, it is a spiritual imperative. Islam teaches us that unresolved resentment poisons the heart and blocks mercy. The Prophet Muhammad (SAW), warned us not to let grudges linger, and that delay in reconciliation has spiritual consequences.

> "The gates of Paradise are opened on Monday and Thursday, and every servant who does not associate anything with Allah is forgiven, except a man who has had an argument with his brother. It is said: 'Wait for these two until they reconcile.'"
>
> The Prophet Muhammad (SAW), Sahih Muslim, 2565

This hadith reminds us that forgiveness from Allah is delayed when we delay forgiving one another. Just as Step Nine urges us to make direct amends wherever possible, Islam urges us to clean our hearts quickly—before the opportunity passes or the damage hardens. Waiting too long to right a wrong doesn't just cost us peace with others. It may cost us access to divine mercy.

The Qur'an reinforces this ethic:

> *"And hasten to forgiveness from your Lord and a garden as wide as the heavens and the earth, prepared for the righteous."*
>
> Qur'an, 3:133

In Islam, part of hastening to Allah's forgiveness includes making amends with others. While Allah may forgive His own rights, the rights of people (*ḥuqūq al-ʿibād*) require us to seek forgiveness from those we have harmed. Whether or not they choose to forgive us is in their hands, and in the hands of Allah. What matters is that we approach them sincerely, clean our side of the street, and do our part in making things right. Insha'Allah, they forgive us. But regardless of the outcome, the act of making amends restores our own integrity and opens the door to divine mercy.

When Prompt Isn't Possible

Sometimes immediate amends aren't wise. For instance, high emotions, necessary privacy, or the need for more reflection prevent immediate amends. In these cases, "prompt" means "as soon," not "instantly." The key is not to let the sun set on your wrongdoing, if you can help it.

By making amends promptly, we develop a spiritual nimbleness; the ability to catch ourselves quickly, admit wrongdoing humbly, and return to alignment with Allah's will. This practice gradually reshapes our character, making us more honest, humble, and accountable in all our affairs.

Respectability and the Paradox of Recovery

Addiction respects nothing. It mocks order, decency, dignity.

In contrast, the further we recover, the more respectful we become. Not performatively, but sincerely. We spoke more carefully. Walk more gently. Listen more fully.

We live with *adab*: refined character, spiritual courtesy.

Not because we've perfected ourselves—but because we remember what it felt like to be lost. And we don't want to go back.

We're not just trying to avoid relapse anymore. We're becoming people others can trust. People whose words mean something. People who reflect, however dimly, the mercy that pulled us from the fire.

The Continuous Cycle of Recovery

Step Ten doesn't stand alone. It is the ongoing, daily expression of all the steps that came before it, starting with Step One. And I cannot stress this enough: every single one of us wakes up each morning with untreated alcoholism. What kept us sober yesterday might not be enough to keep us sober today.

I've slipped before, more than once, because I got complacent. I stopped doing the work. The Big Book warns us not to rest on our laurels, but it is incredibly easy to fall into spiritual arrogance, especially when we have some clean time under our belt. I have relapsed after multiple years of sobriety, and I can tell you from lived experience: the only thing we truly have is today.

Each of us in recovery woke up this morning with untreated alcoholism. The only thing we are promised is a daily reprieve, contingent on the maintenance of our spiritual condition. Step Ten is how we perform that maintenance. We are going to grow. We are going to evolve as people. Our program needs to evolve with us. What worked in the past may not be enough now. Since we only have today, we stay sober by taking personal inventory, keeping our character defects in check, and staying humble.

One year, two years, ten years—none of it matters if we are not maintaining our spiritual condition. That is the truth. Recovery is not something we finish. It is a daily practice. A way of living that depends on constant spiritual attention. Step Ten is the tool we use to stay connected. We use it thoroughly, honestly, vigilantly, and with compassion.

When practiced daily, Step Ten activates a continuous cycle of spiritual growth. It keeps our recovery dynamic and alive.

The Continuous Cycle in Action

- Step One in Daily Life: We remember we are powerless without Allah's help and that our lives become unmanageable when we drift from that truth.

- Step Two in Daily Life: We continually renew our trust that a Power greater than ourselves can restore us to sanity.

- Step Three in Daily Life: We reaffirm our decision to turn our will and our lives over to the care of Allah—again and again.

- Step Four in Daily Life: We inventory ourselves in real time, noticing fear, resentment, selfishness, or dishonesty as they arise.

- Step Five in Daily Life: We admit our wrongs promptly, maintaining honesty with ourselves, with others, and with Allah.

- Step Six in Daily Life: We become willing—again and again—to have our character defects removed as they resurface.

- Step Seven in Daily Life: We humbly ask Allah to remove those defects each time we notice them.

- Steps Eight and Nine in Daily Life: We become willing to make amends for new harms, and we follow through without delay.

This isn't a checklist. It's a living rhythm. A feedback loop that keeps us spiritually awake. We identify, admit, become willing, ask for help, and make amends. And through this process, we change. Slowly, steadily, and by the will of Allah.

In Islamic terms, this reflects the ongoing journey of *tazkiyah* (purification) and *tawbah* (repentance). As said:

> "By Allah, I seek forgiveness from Allah and turn to Him in repentance more than seventy times a day."
>
> Prophet Muhammad (SAW), Sahih al-Bukhari, 6307

Even the Messenger of Allah (SAW), whose heart was pure, modeled constant return to God. That should tell us something.

Step Ten asks us to be persistent. Recovery isn't about never slipping; it's about recognizing when we do and correcting our course quickly. Here is our mechanism for immediate correction. Not later. Not next week. Now.

That's what daily spiritual maintenance is about: keeping things from falling apart before they do. Catching the resentment before it becomes rage. Catching the ego before it becomes isolation. It's the difference between maintenance and repair. One keeps you grounded. The other tries to pull you out of a ditch.

The Big Book clearly states: we are not cured. We have a daily reprieve, contingent on the maintenance of our spiritual condition.

The Nightly Review: Traditional *Muhasaba*

While spot-check inventories happen throughout the day, the nightly review is a dedicated practice of reflection and realignment. This practice has deep roots in both recovery and Islamic tradition.

In recovery, the *Big Book* suggests we "continue to watch for selfishness, dishonesty, resentment, and fear," and when these crop up, "we ask God at once to remove them" (p. 84).

We arrive again at the practice of *muhasaba*. This time, the nightly self-accounting recommended by scholars through the centuries.

A Structured Approach to Nightly Review

1. Begin with gratitude - What blessings did I receive today? How was I helped or guided?

2. Review your actions - How did I treat others? Where did I fall short of my ideals? Where did Allah help me do better than I might have?

3. Examine your heart - What emotions dominated today? What triggered me? What am I carrying that needs to be released?

4. Identify needed amends - Who deserves an apology or correction from me tomorrow?

5. Plan constructive action - What specific steps will I take to address any issues I've identified?

6. Surrender to Allah - Release the day's failures and successes alike into Allah's hands, trusting His mercy and guidance.

This nightly practice becomes a spiritual habit. Allowing us to process the day's events, learn from our missteps, release what needs to be released, and enter sleep with a clean heart. It prevents the accumulation of resentments, guilt, and spiritual debris that could eventually lead us back to active addiction.

Like the sailor who checks his navigational charts each night to ensure he's still on course, our nightly review helps us maintain our spiritual bearing, making slight corrections before we drift too far from our intended path.

A Personal Journey Through Step Ten

In the rooms of recovery, we often hear the phrase: "Our disease is out in the parking lot doing push ups while we're sitting in a meeting." It's a vivid reminder that addiction doesn't take a day off. It's patient. It's persistent. And it's always looking for an opening.

Islam offers a parallel understanding. Whether it is the influence of *shayṭān* or even our own *nafs*, the evil that whispers selfishness and invites destruction is always near. Just like the disease of addiction, *shayṭān* doesn't barge in with drama. He waits. He lingers. He circles quietly, looking for weakness. We could just as easily say: while we're inside praying, *shayṭān* is outside doing push-ups.

> *"Indeed, Shayṭān is an enemy to you, so take him as an enemy."*
>
> Qur'an, 35:6

Step Ten is how I stay aware of this reality. Because I've lived long enough to know slips don't start with catastrophes. They start with little compromises. A flicker of resentment. A missed *ṣalāh*. A half-truth. A small, selfish act that doesn't get addressed. And before you know it, you're drifting. That drift can become a disaster if you don't catch it in time. Complacency kills.

The irony is that the complacency isn't even intentional when it first begins. Many years ago, at the start of my first iteration in sobriety, I was down to zero in my life. I was broke, unemployed, and facing homelessness. I had managed to beg, borrow, or steal just enough to keep feeding my addiction while also burning bridges like it was an Olympic sport. When I finally hit bottom and dragged myself to that first meeting, there was nothing else left. My program became my life. I went to meetings every single day, sometimes more than one a day. I was always on the phone with a fellow recovering addict. The Fellowship and the Steps were my entire world.

> "Heedlessness is the root of every sin. When the heart becomes blind to
> its own faults, the soul becomes proud, and the path to God is forgotten."
>
> Imam al-Ghazali, Iḥyā' 'Ulūm al-Dīn

But gradually, as my sobriety grew, I started getting things back. I found a job, and that took up more of my time. Not long after that, I enrolled in college. After a year of being clean, I entered a relationship. (For the record, I know that is *ḥarām*, but this was before I accepted Islam.) The more life I added outside the rooms, the less time I spent inside them. Daily meetings became every other day. Then, once a week. Phone calls turned into texts. I talked to my sponsor less and less.

I stayed busy, but it was the wrong kind of busy. I was busy with the *dunya* when I should have been busy with God. My complacency with my sobriety weakened my spiritual condition. Before too long, I found myself in a place I shouldn't have been, around people I shouldn't have been associating with. And once again, I found myself with a bottle in my hand and a pipe in my mouth. All because I wasn't doing what I was supposed to be doing. I threw away three years of sobriety because, slowly but surely, I was living selfishly again.

Thankfully, I made it back to the rooms, but it took hitting another bottom to get there. The things I should have been grateful for, I took for granted. I became less present, less grounded. That slow spiritual degradation was the crack in the armor my disease needed to grab hold again.

> "Beware of the whisperings that arrive like guests but settle like masters.
> If you do not shut the door of your heart with remembrance, they will
> furnish your soul with forgetfulness."
>   Attributed to Shaykh Abū Madyan al-Ghawth

Islam names this force *waswās*, the slinking whisperer. The subtle voice that quietly suggests betrayal of what you know is right. I've always called it Death's Radio—that internal static, the background murmur that says, "Why not just give in?" It doesn't shout. It whispers. And the whisper, if entertained, becomes a narrative. A justification. A permission slip to destroy yourself slowly.

Step Ten is how I answer back. Not with panic, but with presence. It teaches me to stay awake, to watch the state of my heart, the shape of my thinking, and the direction of my behavior. It doesn't mean I'm flawless. It means I'm honest. Honest enough to admit when I've slipped. Humble enough to clean it up. Quick enough to fix it before it grows.

Recovery has taught me that the worst damage I've done didn't come from colossal failures. It came from ignoring small ones. Thinking they didn't matter. Believing I had time. I know better now.

Step Ten is a safeguard. It's daily spiritual patrol. Not because we live in fear, but because we've seen what happens when we stop paying attention.

This is a survival instruction. Whether we call it addiction, ego, or the whispering devil, we are told clearly: do not take this threat lightly.

So I don't. I try to stay honest. I try to stay humble. And I try to stay close to the truth of my condition: that without constant awareness, I fall asleep at the wheel. And when I fall asleep, Death's Radio gets louder.

Balancing Vigilance with Self-Compassion

Step Ten calls for continuous inventory and prompt admission of wrongs. A practice that requires consistent monitoring. But without proper balance, vigilance can become harsh self-scrutiny or even self-punishment. Therefore self-compassion is an essential companion to Step Ten.

When Vigilance Becomes Harmful

- When it turns into obsessive self-monitoring

- When it's motivated by fear rather than love

- When it leads to shame rather than growth

- When it becomes a tool of the ego rather than the spirit

"Allah is gentle and loves gentleness in all matters."
Prophet Muhammad (SAW), Sahih al-Bukhari, Hadith 6927

This applies not just to how we treat others, but to how we treat ourselves.

Islamic Framework for Self-Compassion

In Islamic tradition, Allah has 99 Names—each reflecting a Divine attribute that offers both insight and guidance. These Names are not only ways to know Allah but also invitations to embody His qualities in how we relate to ourselves and others.

- *Ar-Rahman* (The Most Compassionate) — We can be compassionate with our humanity.

- *Al-Ghaffar* (The Oft-Forgiving) — We can forgive our mistakes rather than dwell on them

- *As-Sabur* (The Most Patient) — We can be patient with our growth process

- *Al-Wadud* (The Most Loving) — emphasizes Allah's loving nature along with mercy; useful when you want to convey warmth and gentleness.

Practical Application

When practicing Step Ten, consider:

1. Am I being as gentle with myself as Allah is with me?

2. Would I speak to a beloved friend the way I'm speaking to myself?

3. Am I confusing self-improvement with self-criticism?

4. Am I recognizing progress alongside shortcomings?

Self-compassion isn't self-indulgence. It's not making excuses or avoiding accountability. Rather, it's bringing the same mercy to ourselves that we hope to receive from Allah.

There's wisdom in the saying: *"We're not responsible for our disease, but we are responsible for our recovery."* This balanced perspective allows us to hold ourselves accountable without shame, to practice vigilance without punishment, and to grow spiritually without self-abuse.

Step Ten practiced with self-compassion, becomes sustainable. Rather than a burden we eventually abandon, it becomes a practice of loving self-care that nourishes our recovery for a lifetime.

Tools of the Watchful Traveler

1. **The Sacred Pause**—Spiritual maturity lives in the pause. The breath between urge and reaction. This is where you find Allah's mercy waiting. Stop. Breathe. Say, Ya Allah, guide me in this moment. Let that one breath shift your day.

2. **Spot-Check Inventory**—When something feels off, pause and check in. Ask: What's really bothering me? This moment... or something deeper? Watch for

patterns. Ask Allah to remove what does not serve Him.

3. **Prompt Admission of Wrongdoing**—When you're wrong, admit it. Don't wait. Say it to the person. Say it to your sponsor. Say it to Allah. Keep your heart clean. Keep your record short. Move on, lighter.

4. **Nightly Review**—Every night, five minutes. Where did I align with Allah today? Where did I drift? What needs adjusting before tomorrow? Whisper it in prayer. Write it down. Speak it in the dark. This is how you steer your soul.

5. **Spiritual Conditioning**—You're not hypersensitive; you're waking up. A sharp word stings. Idle scrolling leaves a shadow. You feel it. That's a gift. That's awareness. Ask: Does this bring me closer to Allah? That's your compass.

6. **Accountability and Fellowship**—Share your inner life. Not all of it—but some of it. With someone you trust. The disease thrives in isolation. Recovery flourishes in connection. We need each other to stay clear.

"Indeed, those who are mindful of Allah—when an impulse touches them from Satan—they remember [Him], and at once they regain clear insight."
                                                                    Qur'an, 7:201

Mindfulness empowers us to catch ourselves quickly when wrong impulses arise — returning to awareness of Allah (God-consciousness) is how we restore clear vision before harm is done.

Reflection Questions – Chapter Ten

1. When I experience emotional disturbance or tension, what is it usually pointing to within me that needs attention or change?

2. How does pausing for reflection throughout the day help me return to sincerity, humility, and presence with Allah?

3. In what ways has taking a daily inventory helped me repair my conduct more quickly and respond to life with greater compassion?

Continuous culmination

As we integrate Step Ten into our daily lives, our foundation becomes increasingly stable. The preventative maintenance of ongoing inventory and prompt amends keeps our spiritual condition strong and our recovery resilient.

This step marks a transition in our recovery journey. The intensive inner work of the first nine steps leads to daily practices that maintain and deepen our spiritual awakening. With newfound tools, greater awareness, and a commitment to ongoing care, we live with consistency and intention.

Step Ten does not intend to induce anxiety or obsession with its vigilance. Rather, it offers the peace that comes from knowing we're attentive to our spiritual condition. We're no longer at the mercy of unexamined thoughts, hidden resentments, or festering guilt. We have a practice, a way of life, that allows us to live with clarity and purpose.

When we slip, as we all do, we have a method for returning to balance. We don't need to wait until we've spiraled out or reached another bottom. We can make small, consistent corrections that keep us aligned with Allah's will for us.

As we move toward Step Eleven, we carry with us the understanding that recovery isn't a destination, but a journey. One that requires ongoing awareness, honest self-reflection, and prompt correction. With Step Ten as our daily practice, we're prepared to deepen our conscious contact with Allah through prayer and meditation, equipped with the clean heart that makes spiritual connection possible.

The Prophet Muhammad (SAW) said, "Whoever knows himself, knows his Lord." Through the practice of Step Ten, we come to know ourselves more honestly, more compassionate, and more completely. In doing so, we draw closer to knowing Allah.

Our journey continues, one day at a time, one inventory at a time, one sincere amend at a time. And with each cycle of awareness and correction, we move forward more freely, more serene, and more purposefully on the path of recovery.

Chapter Eleven

Dynamic Serenity

S tep Eleven invites us to listen with our hearts. We feel subtle. movement. The guidance of God rarely arrives in dramatic ways. More often, it's subtle, like wind.

Air in motion is invisible, yet powerful enough to change landscapes. It moves quietly through open spaces, yet can carry seeds, shift weather, and sustain life across the globe. This is how divine guidance often works. We receive through small impressions, gentle nudges, and inner clarity. As we increase our conscious contact with the Creator through practices like *Dhkir*, we can notice and respond to these gentle signs.

In Islamic belief, the breath is more than a biological function. Allah says,

> *"And He breathed into him of His spirit..."* (Qur'an, 38:72).

This refers to the *ruh*, the soul, or spirit that gives us life. That Divine breath continues through every human generation, and ultimately, it connects all of us.

Unlike land or sea, nothing divides the air. It surrounds and connects everyone. The same atmosphere flows over distant nations, through cities and forests, across conflict zones and peaceful homes alike. It doesn't distinguish. It unites.

Practicing Step Eleven means realizing this connection. Prayer and meditation are not about calling God down from somewhere far away. They are about quieting ourselves enough to notice what's already present. The Almighty is as near as our heart.

We're not trying to hear a voice. We're learning to recognize direction. The goal isn't dramatic inspiration; it's alignment.

When we stop chasing and start listening, we often find the clarity we were missing.

Step 11: Sought through prayer and meditation to improve our conscious contact with God as we understood Him, praying only for knowledge of His will for us and the power to carry that out.

Big Book of Alcoholics Anonymous (4th Edition):

- "As we go through the day we pause, when agitated or doubtful, and ask for the right thought or action." -p. 87

- "We usually conclude the period of meditation with a prayer that we be shown all through the day what our next step is to be, that we be given whatever we need to take care of such problems." -p. 87

- "What used to be the hunch or the occasional inspiration gradually becomes a working part of the mind." -p. 87

Twelve Steps and Twelve Traditions:

- "Prayer and meditation are our principal means of conscious contact with God." -p. 96

- "The actual point is that sometimes we think we are asking God's will when in fact we are asking to expand our own comfort zone." -p. 102

- "The attitude of prayer and meditation is one of humility and devotion." -p. 97

Qur'anic Reference:

"And those who strive for Us—We will surely guide them to Our paths. And indeed, Allah is with the doers of good." (Qur'an, 29:69)

The Silence That Speaks

In active addiction, silence was often something we avoided. Stillness gave rise to discomfort. It left room for guilt, regret, and fear to surface. So we filled the space with noise, externally and internally. Blaring music, running the TV in the background, or simply muttering to yourself, we would do anything to fill that void with noise, no matter what it was.

Spiritual growth requires us to reclaim that space. Growth asks us to embrace the stillness.

Step Eleven directs us toward prayer and meditation. By the time we get to this point in our recovery, we know these are more than abstract concepts. These are disciplines. Practices. Ways of showing up daily for the relationship we now have with our Creator. They are how we learn to listen, first with our ears and beyond with our hearts.

In recovery, we understand that silence is not the absence of God. It is the condition in which awareness of Him becomes possible.

This is the essence of *muraqabah*: spiritual vigilance. More than merely passive observation. Rather an active, alert presence. A disciplined awareness that God sees and knows what is in our hearts, even when we don't.

> *"And know that Allah knows what is within yourselves, so beware of Him."*
>
> Qur'an, 2:235

Meditation in the AA context is not about achieving a mystical state or emptying the mind. It is about becoming still enough to recognize our thoughts, to examine our motives, and to create space for Divine guidance. We are not trying to hear a voice. We are trying to align with the will of The One who already knows what is best for us.

The goal of Step Eleven is not emotional comfort. We seek instead to cultivate spiritual clarity.

We ask God simply for knowledge of His will and the power to carry it out. That request requires us to get quiet enough to recognize the difference between our will and His. Silence becomes a necessary condition of obedience.

My sponsor often says, "Prayer is when you talk to God; meditation is when you listen." One is an act of speaking; the other, of receiving. Together, they form the foundation of a genuine relationship with the Divine Presence, one that flows both ways.

Conscious contact means paying attention to Allah. On purpose, with presence. It grows through consistency, not drama.

Prayer, Supplication, and Spiritual Presence in Islam

In the Islamic tradition, prayer is not merely a spiritual tool. Prayer is a foundational obligation and a direct line to the Divine.

> *"Establish prayer for My remembrance."*
>
> Qur'an, 20:14

The formal prayer, *ṣalāh*, is the cornerstone of spiritual practice. It is precise, disciplined, and timed. We do not invent its form or content. The Prophet (SAW) received it through revelation and conveyed it through his example. It is how we fulfill the command to "remember Allah much" with our body, tongue, and heart in alignment.

Remember, Step Eleven is more than just ritual prayer. It includes supplication (*du'ā*) and meditative presence (*muraqabah*). Both of which are richly rooted in our tradition.

In Islam, we begin with *ṣalāh*. The ritual prayer, which opens the door to the Divine Presence.

To prepare for this, we enter a state of *wudu*. *Wudu* (ablution) is the sacred act of preparing oneself to stand before Allah in prayer. It is more than a physical washing; it is a spiritual cleansing, a way of removing the distractions and impurities of the world before entering a direct conversation with the Divine. Performing *wudu* reminds us that prayer is not something to be approached casually; it requires intention, purity, and presence. Just as we cleanse our bodies outwardly, we are also preparing our hearts inwardly to meet our Lord with humility and sincerity. The appendix contains a short guide to *wudu* for those unfamiliar with this practice.

> "We shouldn't be shy on this matter of prayer. Better men than we are using it constantly. It works if we have the proper attitude and work at it."

Alcoholics Anonymous, p. 85

And at the heart of every unit of prayer is *Surah Al-Fātiḥah*, the Opening. The spiritual key. When we recite it, we affirm *tawḥīd*, we acknowledge our dependence, and we ask for guidance. This is not a performance for God; it is a preparation of the self. The act of standing, bowing, and prostrating aligns the body with the heart, and the heart with the will of Allah. Only after opening that door. Only after we have said, "You alone we worship, and You alone we ask for help, ", do we move into *du'ā*, our personal supplication. Because in this tradition, we do not shout across a distance. We knock, and then we speak.

Du'ā: Intimate Supplication

Du'ā is informal, personal, and relational. It is the act of turning to Allah in our own words, with our own needs, from wherever we are. You can whisper it before sleep, utter it in the driver's seat, or speak it silently in your heart during a moment of doubt.

> "Du'ā is worship."
> Prophet Muhammad (SAW), Jami' at-Tirmidhi 3372

This means that every sincere request directed toward Allah is an act of submission and devotion. It trains the heart to recognize its dependence and to expect from the Source of all provision.

In recovery, we learn to make *du'ā* not only in moments of crisis, but as part of daily spiritual maintenance. We ask Allah:

- To guide our decisions

- To remove our defects

- To protect us from self-will

- To make us useful to others

- To fill our hearts with gratitude

This is Step Eleven in action: asking only for knowledge of His will and the power to carry that out.

Muraqabah: Watchfulness and Inner Alignment

The word *muraqabah* connotes watchfulness, guarding, and attentiveness.

In Islamic theology, *muraqabah* refers to the spiritual state of being aware that Allah sees you. It directly results from *ihsan* as described in the Hadith Jibril:

> "*Ihsan* is to worship Allah as though you see Him; and though you do not see Him, know that He sees you."
>
> Prophet Muhammad (SAW), Sahih Muslim 8Prophet Muhammad
> (SAW), Sahih Muslim 8

This is ethical and spiritual accountability. This active discipline stems from the awareness that we are always in the presence of our Creator, who constantly observes our intentions and actions.

When practiced alongside *du'ā* and *ṣalāh*, *muraqabah* becomes a powerful spiritual orientation. It increases humility, deepens sincerity, and anchors our emotional responses in Divine presence rather than ego reaction.

Spiritual Practices as Recovery Tools

These Islamic spiritual practices are more than religious obligations, they're practical recovery tools that directly address the challenges of addiction:

- *Salāh* (ritual prayer) creates structure and routine that counters the chaos of addiction

- *Wudu* (ablution) serves as a physical ritual that can interrupt craving cycles

- *Dhikr* (remembrance) provides an immediate spiritual alternative when thoughts of substance abuse arise

- *Muraqabah* (watchfulness) develops the awareness to recognize triggers before they lead to use

- *Du'ā* (supplication) gives us a way to acknowledge vulnerability without surrendering to it

Before I accepted Islam, I was praying the way AA had taught me. Wakeup, pray up, and start the day. Ask God to help me stay sober. At night, thank Him for getting me through. In AA, maintaining sobriety was the central focus of most prayers—and rightly so. It's Alcoholics Anonymous. That kind of prayer kept me sober. But even then, I felt like something was missing.

It wasn't until I entered Islam that I truly understood the blessing of prayer. I realized it was more than asking Allah for help with sobriety. When the call to prayer sounds, it is an invitation to unplug from the *dunya* and reconnect with the Divine. No matter what I am doing, when I hear the *adhan*, I stop and recognize that this moment is a gift. Praying *ṣalāh* with brothers at the *masjid* deepened my connection to Allah and strengthened my sense of spiritual fellowship, offering a purity that complements the community found in AA.

I don't see pr as something I have to do. I see it as something I get to do. There are many souls in the *barzakh* who would give anything to come back and perform even one *rak'ah*. We are blessed to still have this chance.

> "Recite what has been revealed to you of the Book and establish prayer. Surely prayer restrains from indecency and wrongdoing. And the remembrance of Allah is greater. And Allah knows what you do."
>
> Qur'an, 29:45

In AA, prayer often bookends the day. In Islam, prayer structures the entire day. One thing I immediately loved about Islam was how the time between each *ṣalāh* becomes shorter as the day goes on. There are several hours between *Fajr* and *Dhuhr*, then a shorter time until *'Asr*, then even less between *'Asr* and *Maghrib*, and the shortest gap between Maghrib and *Ishā'*. That rhythm struck me from the beginning. It felt like a built-in resistance to the pull of the dunya. As the world's influence grows stronger, Allah calls us back to Him with greater frequency.

Ṣalāh is my spiritual reset. It realigns my heart with Allah. In my experience, recovery with Islam is far easier than a secular recovery model. Instead of taking it one day at a time, I stay sober one *ṣalāh* at a time. Each prayer helps me discern Allah's will, giving me strength to stay sober.

A Daily Recovery Framework with the Five Prayers

Step Eleven calls us to consistent practice, not occasional inspiration. In Islam, the five daily prayers (*salah*) provide a divinely ordained structure for conscious contact with Allah throughout the day. To make *salah* and *dhikr* practical recovery tools, here's a framework to weave them into daily life:

Pre-Dawn: *Fajr*

Prayer and Morning Practice (30-45 minutes)

1. Rise with intention—Wake for *Fajr* by setting your *niyyah* (intention): "I rise seeking Allah's pleasure and guidance for this day."

2. Purification—Perform *wudu* mindfully, feeling each rinse as both a physical and spiritual cleansing.

3. *Fajr* prayer—Approach the first prayer with full presence. Feel the transition from darkness to light, from sleep to awakening consciousness.

4. Post-prayer *dhikr*—Remain seated after prayer for morning remembrance: *Subhan'Allah, Alhamdulillah, Allahu Akbar.*

5. Qur'anic reflection—Read even a brief passage of the Qur'an after *Fajr*, allowing the words to settle in your heart.

6. Morning *du'a*—Ask specifically: "Allah, show me Your will for me today. Give me strength to follow it and resist temptation."

7. Silent contemplation—Sit in quiet receptivity for 5-10 minutes, training yourself to listen for divine guidance. **Mid-Day: *Dhuhr***

Prayer and Recovery Check-in (15-20 minutes)

1. Mindful break—Pause from daily activities, transitioning from worldly concerns to divine connection.

2. Renew *wudu*—Use this physical cleansing as a chance to reset mentally and spiritually.

3. *Dhuhr* prayer—Pray with the awareness that you're stepping out of the day's chaos into sacred time.

4. Brief *dhikr*—After prayer, repeat "*Astaghfirullah*" (I seek Allah's forgiveness) to clear the heart of morning missteps.

5. Recovery check-in—Ask yourself: "Am I maintaining my spiritual condition? Have I acted from self-will this morning?"

6. Course correction—How is your heart? How is your mood? If adjustments to your disposition and attitude are necessary, make them honestly.

Afternoon: *Asr*

Prayer and Gratitude Practice (15-20 minutes)

1. Intentional pause—As the day's activities peak, consciously step away to reconnect with Allah.

2. *Asr* prayer—Pray with attention to the changing light, recognizing time's passage and life's impermanence.

3. Gratitude check up—After prayer, identify three specific blessings received so far today.

4. Brief *dhikr*—Repeat "*Alhamdulillah*" (All praise belongs to Allah) with each blessing in mind.

5. Renewal of intention—Realign your thoughts and actions with the will of Allah as the day continues.

Sunset: *Maghrib*

Prayer and Reflection (20-30 minutes)

1. Transitional awareness—Use the day's beginning as a natural boundary for reflection.

2. *Maghrib* prayer—Pray with awareness of the new day, surrendering its outcomes to Allah.

3. Post-prayer Qur'an—Read Surah *Al-Falaq* and *An-Nas* as protection for the evening hours.

4. Daily review—Conduct a brief inventory: Where did I feel Allah's guidance today? Where did I resist it?

5. Evening *du'a*—Ask Allah for protection from evening temptations, when many relapses occur.

Night: *Isha*

Prayer and Closing Practice (30-45 minutes)

1. Final purification—Perform *wudu* intending to cleanse the day's spiritual dust.

2. *Isha* prayer—Approach the night prayer as a completion of the day's spiritual cycle.

3. Extended *dhikr*—Engage in remembrance of Allah's names or phrases from the *Sunnah*.

4. Bedtime *du'a*—Recite the prophetic bedtime supplications, adding personal prayers for continued recovery.

5. Gratitude and surrender—Release the day's events, outcomes, and concerns into Allah's care.

6. Intention setting—Set your intention to begin tomorrow with a renewed commitment to spiritual practice.

Voluntary Prayers (*Nawafil*) to Strengthen Recovery

Beyond the five obligatory prayers, voluntary prayers offer additional opportunities to deepen your spiritual connection and strengthen your recovery.

Tahajjud (Night Prayer)

The quiet hours before dawn provide a uniquely powerful time for spiritual connection.

> *"The closest that the Lord is to His servant is in the last part of the night, so if you can be among those who remember Allah at that time, then do so."*
> Prophet Muhammad (SAW), Sunan al-Tirmidhi 3579

For those in recovery, *Tahajjud* offers:
- Solitude for deeper self-examination when distractions are minimized

- Spiritual protection during vulnerable nighttime hours when relapse thoughts may arise

- A private space to speak honestly to Allah about anything

Recovery Practice: During *Tahajjud*, focus one *rak'ah* specifically on your recovery journey. After reciting Surah Al-Fatiha, add Surah Ad-Duha, which speaks beautifully of Allah's care during difficult times.

Duha (Mid-Morning Prayer)

This prayer, offered after sunrise when the day begins in earnest, serves as a spiritual anchor during busy mornings.

For recovery, *Duha* provides:

- A mid-morning spiritual reset when stress builds

- Protection during the transition from home to work/social environments

- A reminder of spiritual priorities before daily demands take over

Recovery Practice: Make *Duha* a regular practice before leaving home or starting work, especially if mornings were previously associated with using or drinking.

Istikhara (Prayer for Guidance)

This special prayer for divine guidance is valuable for those in recovery facing tough decisions.

When recovery brings challenging choices about relationships, work, or amends, *Istikhara* offers:

- A structured way to seek Allah's guidance rather than relying on self-will

- Protection from impulsive decisions that might threaten sobriety

- Patience to wait for clarity rather than rushing into action

Recovery Practice: Before making significant recovery-related decisions, perform *Istikhara* and remain attentive to signs of guidance in the following days.

Salat at-Tawba (Prayer of Repentance)

This two-*rak'ah* prayer, specifically focused on repentance, provides spiritual cleansing when guilt or shame arises.

For recovery, this prayer offers:

- Immediate spiritual relief when thoughts of past actions become overwhelming

- A constructive alternative to shame spirals that might trigger relapse

- A way to practice Step Ten's principle of prompt admission

Recovery Practice: When memories of active addiction create shame, or when you make a mistake in recovery, perform *Salat at-Tawba* followed by sincere *du'a* for continued healing. Remember, we should never despair of Allah's mercy, for He says:

> *"Say, 'O My servants who have transgressed against themselves [through sin], do not despair of the mercy of Allah. Indeed, Allah forgives all sins."*
>
> Qur'an, 39:53

For Moments of Craving or Temptation

When the desire for substances arises, immediately:

1. Perform *wudu* as a physical interruption of craving

2. Pray two *rak'ahs* of voluntary prayer, even if very brief

3. Recite "*La hawla wa la quwwata illa billah*" (There is no might nor power except with Allah)

4. Physically change your location, if possible

5. Call a sponsor or recovery support person

When I feel myself slipping, mentally, emotionally, or spiritually, making *wudu* helps immensely. The simple act of washing, especially when that cold water touches my face, grounds me immediately. It's as if I'm rinsing away the heaviness, the negativity, the static. And I am. *Wudu* isn't just ritual; its spiritual realignment. There's a reason it's required in Islam, and I encourage anyone, even non-Muslims, to try it and experience the clarity it brings.

Remember that the goal isn't perfect practice, but sincere connection. Allah responds to the heart's intention more than to perfect form.

> *"Allah does not look at your forms or your wealth, but rather at your hearts and your deeds."*
>
> Prophet Muhammad (SAW), Sahih Muslim 2564

Meditation in Recovery

While the Big Book leaves meditation loosely defined, other AA literature gives us more to work with. *Living Sober* offers this:

> *"It helps to sit quietly for a few moments, concentrate on our breathing, and say the Serenity Prayer slowly to ourselves. This may not seem like 'meditation' to some, but it works for us."*
>
> Living Sober, Chapter 11

Meditation doesn't have to be complicated. It can be as simple as sitting still, breathing, and bringing our attention to a spiritual truth. What matters is the intention to pause, listen inwardly, and reconnect with guidance.

This intention mirrors the Islamic practice of *muraqabah*, or spiritual watchfulness. *Muraqabah* means sitting in conscious awareness of Allah—watching the heart, noticing the thoughts that arise, and gently returning to presence. It is not about clearing the mind, but about tuning the heart. It asks, "Where is this thought leading me? Is it aligned with who I want to become?"

> "If the forms of remembrance disappear from your tongue, and you find no pleasure in your practice, then be present with Him through *muraqabah*. Your silence, if attended with awareness of Him, is better than words absent of Him."
>
> Ibn 'Aṭā' Allāh al-Iskandarī, Kitāb al-Ḥikam

Sufi practitioners often pair this with *dhikr*. Others may sit quietly after prayer, simply breathing and focusing on the moment, observing the movements within and seeking alignment with Divine will.

Step Eleven asks us to seek conscious contact with God, and recognizes this as a continuous practice. We pray for knowledge of His Will and for the strength to act on it. That is a clear directive. And it has implications for how we think, speak, move, and respond throughout the day.

> "...we find our thinking will, as time passes, be more and more on the plane of inspiration."
>
> Alcoholics Anonymous, p. 87

We train ourselves to stop before reacting. To reflect before speaking. To pray before deciding.

- Is this my will or God's will?

- Is this ego or sincerity?

- Will this action draw me nearer to Allah or further away?

We do this because we understand that mindful action brings stability, while unexamined impulses often lead to chaos.

> *"Say, 'Indeed, my prayer, my rites of sacrifice, my living and my dying are for Allah, Lord of the worlds."*
>
> Qur'an, 6:162

That is the aim of Step Eleven: to bring every aspect of life into alignment with that truth. To live in such a way that our conduct reflects Divine intention. We live consciously.

We will still fall short. We will still miss the mark. Remember to be kind to yourself when you stumble, we are seeking spiritual progress. Working through prayer and meditation, we create a pattern of returning, again and again, to what is right. And that return, that willingness to course correct in real time, becomes the measure of our spiritual condition.

No one promises us certainty. But we receive guidance. And that guidance begins with a humble heart.

GOD = Good Orderly Direction

The beauty of Step 11 is that it's a roadmap of continuous growth. As our awareness deepens, our gratitude expands, and our relationship with the Creator becomes more intimate. As I increase my conscious contact with Allah, I perceive His signs and presence not just during prayer or meetings, but everywhere: in ordinary moments, on quiet walks, in conversations, even in silence. The more I get out of my way, the more clearly I see Him.

This step doesn't mean I've conquered my *nafs*. It means I've become better equipped to redirect my attention away from myself and toward Him. Consciously. Deliberately. I monitor where my thoughts go, where my attention rests, and where my heart is pointed. And when I'm aware of my orientation, I can shift it—realign it—toward Allah.

> "You were born with wings. Why prefer to crawl through life? Purify your heart, and fly into the presence of the Divine."
>
> Jalāl al-Dīn Rūmī, Mathnawī

So where is my focus? Step 11 invites me to return to that question again and again. We find the miracle by deepening contact with the Divine. We are walking a path that leads beyond this world, toward the ultimate meeting with our Creator in the next life. Each step toward Him brings greater clarity, deeper peace, and a heart more prepared for that eventual return. As I draw closer to Allah, I embody *ihsan*, spiritual excellence, which expresses itself through my *adab*, my *deen*, and the gratitude that fills my heart.

Overcoming Common Obstacles to Step Eleven

Many of us encounter challenges in establishing a consistent prayer and meditation practice. Here are common obstacles and practical approaches to overcome them:

"I don't feel anything when I pray or meditate."

This is perhaps the most common struggle. Remember that spiritual connection isn't primarily about feelings; it's about presence and intention. Some days you may experience profound peace; other days, you may feel nothing at all. The practice is valuable, regardless of the emotional response.

Approach: Focus on showing up consistently rather than seeking specific experiences. Notice subtle shifts in your daily life: increased patience, better decisions, more peace.

Rather than looking for dramatic spiritual feelings, the idea is intention rather than expectation.

"My mind won't stop racing."

A busy mind isn't a sign of failure; it's simply the natural condition we're working with. The goal isn't to eliminate thoughts, but to become less identified with them.

Approach: Use an anchor to gain attention. For example, your breath, a phrase of *dhikr*, or awareness of the body. When you notice your mind wandering, gently return to your anchor without judgment. This returning is, itself, the practice.

"I don't have time."

In our busy lives, finding time for spiritual practice can seem impossible. Yet, this is precisely when we most need the clarity that comes from conscious contact.

Approach: Start with just 5 minutes. Integrate practice into existing routines. Brief moments like while waiting for coffee to brew, during your commute, or before checking your phone in the morning. Remember that quality matters more than quantity.

"I'm not sure if I'm doing it 'right'."

Many of us bring perfectionism into our spiritual practice, believing there's one correct technique or approach.

Approach: Trust the process. The sincerity of your intention matters more than perfect technique. As you continue practicing, your approach will naturally refine. Consult with spiritual guides or sponsors when needed, but avoid comparing your practice to others'.

"I struggle with consistency."

Building any new habit takes time and often includes setbacks.

Approach: If you miss a day (or several), simply begin again without self-judgment. Consider using habit-stacking (attaching prayer to an existing habit like morning coffee) or finding an accountability partner for support.

"My past trauma makes meditation difficult."

For those with trauma histories, silence and stillness can sometimes bring up difficult emotions or memories.

Approach: Begin with grounding practices that help you feel safe in your body—perhaps a walking meditation, breath-focused *dhikr*, or a guided visualization. Work with a trauma-informed therapist alongside your spiritual practice, if possible. Remember that Allah is Al-Latif (The Gentle) and meets you where you are.

Remember that Step Eleven is a lifelong practice, not a destination. The aim isn't perfection but progress, advancing a deeper, conscious contact with Allah through daily effort. As the said,

> *"The most beloved of deeds to Allah are those that are consistent, even if they are small."*
>
> Prophet Muhammad (SAW), Sahih al-Bukhari 6465

The Community Dimension of Spiritual Practice

While Step Eleven emphasizes personal prayer and meditation, community supports and deepens our spiritual growth.

> "The hand of Allah is with the community."
> Prophet Muhammad (SAW), Jami' at-Tirmidhi 2166.

In recovery, this community dimension takes several forms:

Jama'ah Prayer

Praying in congregation multiplies the spiritual benefit of *salah* and reinforces our connection to the *ummah*. Regular attendance at the *masjid* also provides structure and accountability that supports recovery.

Recovery Meetings

Whether in 12-Step groups or other recovery communities, sharing our spiritual journey with others who understand addiction creates a powerful synergy. We have a common saying in recovery, "Meeting makers make it."

Study Circles (*Halaqas*)

Taking part in regular Qur'an or Hadith study deepens our understanding and provides spiritual nourishment. Many recovery-focused *halaqas* now exist specifically for Muslims in recovery. Most AA communities around the world will have Big Book focused meetings or study groups regularly, and I encourage all of you to attend.

Service (*Khidma*)

Serving others—whether in the *masjid*, your homegroup, or in the broader community—is itself a spiritual practice that reinforces our connection to Allah and others.

Spiritual Companionship

The Prophet (SAW) taught us that "a person follows the religion of his close friend." Having companions who support your spiritual growth and recovery is invaluable. This is your support network, and having one is vital to lasting recovery. Whether you are new to recovery or even new to Islam, maintaining contact with your companions is almost as important as maintaining contact with Allah.

> *"Do not cut off one another, do not turn away from one another, do not hate one another, and do not envy one another. Be, O slaves of Allah, brothers. It is not permissible for a Muslim to forsake his brother for more than three days."*
>
> Prophet Muhammad (SAW), Sahih al-Bukhari 6065

Integrating community practice with individual devotion creates a more resilient recovery.

Responding Through the Lens of Will

Step Eleven teaches us to seek knowledge of God's will and the power to carry it out. This directive means we have a responsibility to pause and reflect before we act. Especially in moments where instinct, emotion, or ego might otherwise take the lead.

> "As we go through the day we pause, when agitated or doubtful, and ask for the right thought or action." (*Alcoholics Anonymous*, p. 87)

We live that line, not just admire it. We pause. We ask. We seek alignment with what is right, guided by sincerity and trust in the outcome Allah chooses.

In Islamic terms, this is *tawakkul*. Trust in Allah combined with personal effort. We do not ask to be rescued from decision-making. We ask to be shown the correct course of action, and we commit to following it, even when it challenges our preferences.

The Qur'an offers a model:

> *"And consult with them in affairs. Then, when you have taken a decision, put your trust in Allah. Indeed, Allah loves those who rely upon Him."*
> Qur'an, 3:159

This is what spiritual maturity looks like in action. It is a disciplined way of meeting uncertainty with trust and restraint. It involves the willingness to be redirected, to accept being wrong, and to wait with patience.

There will be days when clarity does not arrive right away. Step Eleven does not guarantee instant answers. It offers access to wisdom greater than our own, to insight rooted in sincerity, and to a Source who sees beyond what we can perceive.

That access depends on our willingness to ask, and our willingness to obey once the path becomes clear.

Step Eleven and Relapse Prevention

The conscious contact we develop through Step Eleven becomes a cornerstone of relapse prevention. When consistently practiced, prayer and meditation create multiple layers of protection against return to use.

Early Warning System

Regular spiritual practice increases our self-awareness, helping us recognize when we're drifting toward danger. When our hearts are properly aligned, we can much more easily identify "stinking thinking" and adjust accordingly.

Decision Filter

The habit of seeking guidance creates a crucial space between trigger and response. This pause is often the difference between impulsive action and considered choice.

Stress Management

Prayer and meditation engage our parasympathetic nervous system, reducing the stress and anxiety that often drive substance use. The physiological benefits complement the spiritual ones.

Purpose and Meaning

Conscious contact with Allah reinforces our sense of purpose beyond immediate gratification. This broader perspective makes momentary cravings less compelling.

Spiritual Shield

The Prophet (SAW) taught specific prayers for protection and strength. Memorizing and regularly reciting these creates a spiritual barrier against negative influences.

When spiritual practice slips, it's not usually followed immediately by a relapse. Instead, look for these warning signs that show increased vulnerability:

- Skipping prayers or rushing through them without presence

- Increasing self-reliance without consulting Allah in decisions

- Avoiding recovery meetings or spiritual gatherings

- Neglecting Qur'an recitation or study

- Rationalization of small compromises ("it's just one missed prayer")

- Return of character defects like anger, pride, or dishonesty

Noticing these signs early allows us to renew our spiritual practice before a physical relapse occurs. As the saying goes, "The time to fix the roof is when the sun is shining."

Building on the Foundation

Step Eleven is deeply connected to all the steps that came before it. Each one prepares the heart to approach prayer and meditation with sincerity and purpose. When we see these connections clearly, we treat prayer and meditation not as separate practices, but as essential parts of the recovery journey.

Connection to Step One (Powerlessness)

In prayer and meditation, we continuously reaffirm our powerlessness. We need guidance beyond our own understanding. Each time we pray, "Show me your Will," we admit that our own will has proven insufficient.

Connection to Steps Two and Three (Higher Power and Surrender)

Step Eleven takes the belief and decision of Steps Two and Three and transforms them into daily practice. It's one thing to decide to turn our will over to Allah; it's another to actively seek His will every day through conscious contact.

Connection to Steps Four through Seven (Inventory and Character)

Prayer and meditation deepen our self-knowledge and humility. Through daily spiritual practice, we continue to recognize character defects as they arise and promptly ask for their removal, extending the work of Steps Four through Seven into daily life. This helps us cultivate and practice *adab* in our lives.

Connection to Steps Eight and Nine (Amends)

Consistent conscious contact helps us maintain the clarity and courage needed to make and live our amends. It helps us recognize new harms promptly and address them before they compound.

Connection to Step Ten (Daily Inventory)

Step Ten asks us to continue taking a personal inventory; Step Eleven provides the spiritual clarity to make that inventory accurate and honest. Our prayers and meditation create the space where true self-examination becomes possible.

In the Islamic tradition, this progression parallels the journey from *islām* (submission) to *īmān* (faith) to *iḥsān* (excellence):

- Steps One through Three establish submission. We surrender to a power greater than ourselves

- Steps Four through Nine develop faith. We act on our beliefs in ways that transform our character and relationships

- Steps Ten through Twelve cultivate excellence. We develop conscious awareness of Allah's presence and align our lives with Divine will

As we practice Step Eleven, we deepen every part of our recovery. Prayer and meditation become a daily renewal of the steps we have taken, grounding us in the principles that continue to bring us new life.

> *"Renew your faith." When asked how, he replied: "Say 'Lā ilāha illa Allah' (There is no god but Allah) frequently."*
> Prophet Muhammad (SAW), Musnad Ahmad 8494

This points to a powerful truth: the renewal of faith and the softening of the heart are rooted in *dhikr*—the remembrance of Allah.

Step Eleven invites us to do exactly this—to establish and maintain conscious contact with our Creator through prayer and meditation. Through *dhikr*, the active remembrance of Allah, Islamic tradition sustains and deepens that contact. These hadith remind us that spiritual vitality isn't found in momentary highs, but in the steady rhythm of remembrance, word by word, breath by breath.

The Evolution of Spiritual Perception

As we practice Step Eleven consistently, our spiritual perception evolves. The step says we "increase our conscious contact" and increase implies growth. This evolution follows a natural progression that many mystics and scholars have recognized across traditions:

1. Intellectual Understanding (*'Ilm*) — Our journey begins with knowledge. We learn about prayer, meditation, and the will of Allah on an intellectual level. We study the concepts, memorize the steps, and grasp the spiritual framework. This kind of knowledge (*'ilm*) is essential; it gives us language, structure, and direction. But it is only the first layer. Knowing about Allah is not the same as knowing Allah. Intellectual understanding alone doesn't transform the heart—it must be followed by action, experience, and sincere engagement.

2. Conscious Practice (*'Amal*)—From understanding, we move to action. This is where knowledge becomes embodied through consistent practice or *'amal*. We establish routines of prayer, meditation, and remembrance, even when the results aren't immediate or emotionally charged. We show up. We follow the guidance, not just when we feel inspired, but especially when we don't. This stage is where discipline takes root and sincerity is tested. It's the bridge between knowing the path and walking it.

3. **States of Awareness (*Ḥāl*)**—With continued practice, moments of spiritual presence begin to emerge, fleeting, yet unmistakable. A sudden stillness during prayer, a sense of being seen by Allah, or a flash of inner clarity. These are known as *ahwāl*, temporary spiritual states gifted by Allah, not produced by our own effort. They remind us that true perception is possible, but not yet anchored. *Ḥāl* is not something we control. It descends unexpectedly, inviting us to witness rather than grasp. It teaches humility and prepares the heart for deeper transformation.

4. Integrated Awareness (*Maqām*)—Over time, what were once fleeting states of presence begin to settle into enduring qualities of the heart. These are known as

maqāmāt, spiritual stations attained through sustained effort and Divine grace. In this stage, awareness becomes more consistent. Prayer evolves from routine to a living encounter. We develop a refined spiritual sensitivity, an intuition grounded not in emotion but in submission and alignment with Divine will. Unlike *ḥāl*, which descends without warning, *maqām* reflects a stable inner transformation: the fruit of conscious striving and Divine response.

By the last stage, conscious contact with Allah is no longer limited to prayer mats or moments of crisis. Instead it permeates every aspect of life. We move beyond practicing spiritual principles as external duties and begin to live them as an inward reality. Our actions, decisions, and responses naturally align with Divine guidance, not because we're forcing them, but because our perception has been transformed.

> *"Worship Allah as though you see Him, and if you do not see Him, then know that He sees you."*
>
> Prophet Muhammad (SAW), Sahih al-Bukhari 50

This is the station of *ihsan*—to live with spiritual excellence, with the awareness that Allah is always present. We move from knowing that He sees us to experiencing His presence directly. This is a living process, not a static state. We move through these five stages again and again, sometimes seeing with clarity, other times losing sight. Each cycle invites us to keep moving forward with sincerity, patience, and trust in the unfolding.

In recovery terms, this mirrors the journey from:

- Understanding the concept of sobriety

- Practicing the tools of recovery

- Experiencing moments of spiritual clarity

- Developing intuitive contact with a Higher Power

- Living in sustained alignment with that Power

What was once fleeting becomes foundational. What was once external becomes internalized.

"What used to be the hunch or the occasional inspiration gradually becomes a working part of the mind."

Alcoholics Anonymous, p. 87

Ultimately, this evolution isn't about spiritual achievement. it's about removing the
veils that obscure what has always been present. Step Eleven doesn't create the connection
with Allah; it reveals it. Through consistent practice, sincere effort, and Divine mercy, we
awaken to the truth that Allah has never been absent. We were simply distracted.

Dhikr: From Recitation to Resonance

Dhikr literally means "remembrance," but real *dhikr* runs deeper than repeating words.
True *dhikr* is resonance—aligning your entire being with Allah. Every atom, every mole-
cule in creation is already doing this, vibrating in constant remembrance. *Dhikr* isn't just
something we say; it's something we become.

The first mistake many of us make is thinking *dhikr* is primarily an intellectual exercise.
It's not. You can study the properties of water for years and still not know what it feels
like to be wet. You have to taste it. You have to step into it. *Dhikr* works the same way. It's
not about knowing of Allah; it's about experiencing His Presence directly.

"*Dhikr* is to the heart what water is to the fish. What happens to the fish
when it is taken out of water?"

Imam Ibn Taymiyyah, al-Wabil al-Sayyib

Reciting with focus carries spiritual benefit, as the words of dhikr hold divine resonance. The deeper transformation begins when remembrance moves from the mind into
the heart. When we stop analyzing and start feeling. When the Name of Allah doesn't just
pass our lips but sinks deep into our chest, into our being. This is the difference between
knowing about honey and actually tasting it.

The practice of *dhikr* starts simply: daily recitation of a basic *wird*: affirmations like the
Shahada, *Istighfar* (asking for forgiveness), *Salawat* (sending blessings on the Prophet
(SAW)), and the Names of Allah. We might sit quietly, repeat them, reflect on them. But
the goal isn't quantity. It's presence. It's resonance. Are we feeling it? Are we vibrating
with it? Or are we just ticking boxes?

"Keep your tongue moist with the remembrance of Allah."

Prophet Muhammad (SAW), Jami' at-Tirmidhi 3375

The shift happens when dhikr moves beyond repetition and becomes a lived connection. The breath becomes a bridge to presence, and the Divine Name becomes a guide that keeps the heart aligned with the light of the Qur'an and the mercy of Allah. It's not about trying harder; it's about surrendering more fully.

Trying is lying. You don't achieve resonance; you relax into it. The more you force it, the more you stay trapped in your mind. And the mind, for most of us, is the real addiction. Always chasing, always analyzing, always doubting. True *dhikr* asks us to let go of that. To leave the storm of thoughts behind and swim in the mercy oceans of Allah.

"Whoever remembers Allah much, love for Allah will be born in his heart."

Shaykh Ibn al-Qayyim, Madarij al-Salikin

Consistency matters. Setting aside sacred moments, such as before dawn or just after dusk helps. Keeping *wudu* if possible, sitting in stillness, letting the Names of Allah wash over us. Start with your tongue, but aim for your heart. Feel the vibration. Become the remembrance itself.

Lastly, and most importantly: enjoy it. Don't consider Dhikr a burden. It's meant to heal, to lighten, to open. Every session of *dhikr* is a chance to step through the veil of self and experience the living Presence of The One who is closer to us than our own souls. We're not working to earn that closeness. It's already there. We're just waking up to it.

Dhikr as a Recovery Tool

For those recovering from substance abuse, *dhikr* offers a powerful alternative to the mind-altering substances we once depended on.

The rhythmic nature of *dhikr* has a physiological impact that directly counters cravings. Studies have shown that repetitive spiritual practices can:

• Release endorphins that improve mood naturally

- Lower cortisol levels, reducing stress

- Regulate breathing patterns, calming the nervous system

- Create new neural pathways that support recovery

When cravings arise, having a specific *dhikr* phrase ready—like *"Hasbunallahu wa ni'mal wakeel"* (Allah is sufficient for us, and He is the best guardian)—provides an immediate spiritual alternative that becomes more powerful with regular practice.

Spiritual Dryness

Not every prayer feels meaningful. Not every meditation brings clarity. Sometimes, spiritual practice feels dry, mechanical, or even hollow. Islamic tradition calls this state *qabd*, a state of spiritual contraction. It's not failure; it's part of the path.

Often, spiritual dryness sets in when the *dunya,* the distractions, attachments, and anxieties of this world, begin to occupy the space that belongs to the heart. When our attention shifts from the Eternal to the temporary, from the Creator to the creation, we find our connection weakened. Maintenance of spiritual condition requires vigilance, and when we allow *dunya* to creep in unchecked, it clouds our awareness of Allah.

Understanding Spiritual Dryness

Periods of dryness are not signs of abandonment or punishment. They can serve multiple purposes:

1. Testing our sincerity – Will we keep showing up even when the emotional reward fades?

2. Deepening our humility – Reminding us that spiritual connection is a gift, not something we can manufacture.

3. Breaking our attachment to feelings – Teaching us to seek Allah, not just the comfort that sometimes accompanies worship.

4. Preparing us for deeper growth – Just as physical muscles grow through resistance, the soul strengthens through perseverance.

Even the Prophet Muhammad (SAW) experienced alternating states: moments of intense closeness (*waṣl*) and periods when revelation ceased. The greatest saints and scholars, from the early companions to the later *awliya*, all reported cycles of expansion and contraction. What set them apart was their steadfastness through the spiritual drought.

Spiritual Dryness in Recovery

In recovery, these phases can be especially dangerous. The thought creeps in: "This isn't working, so why bother?" That lie can crack the door open to relapse. But dryness is not the end of the road. Here's how to walk through it:

1. Keep the structure, even without feeling – Continue your routine of prayer, *dhikr*, and meditation. Let your body lead your heart when your spirit feels unmotivated.

2. Return to community – Attend meetings, pray in the *masjid*, or just be around others on the path. The group's collective presence can reignite your individual spark.

3. Simplify – When your spiritual load feels heavy, return to the basics: five daily prayers, short Qur'an recitations, simple *dhikr* like *Subhanallah* and *Alhamdulillah*.

4. Serve others – When your own connection feels dry, helping others can restore meaning and reconnect you to your purpose.

5. Practice gratitude deliberately – Write down three blessings every day, no matter how small. Gratitude shifts your focus back to what is real and sacred.

6. Be raw in your *du'a* – Don't fake feelings. Tell Allah the truth: "I feel distant. I feel numb. But I'm still showing up. Guide me back." That honesty is the connection.

Spiritual dryness is seasonal. Like winter, it strips things bare, but only to make room for spring. If you stay consistent through the silence, the light always returns. What emerges on the other side is not shallow emotion, but a more mature, resilient faith, one that can weather the highs and lows of life and recovery alike.

Cultural Contexts and Recovery

While the spiritual principles of Step Eleven are universal, their expression varies across cultural contexts. Muslims in recovery come from diverse backgrounds; Arab, South Asian, African, Turkish, Indonesian, and Western converts, many others, each with their own cultural approaches to spirituality.

These cultural variations can enrich our understanding of Step Eleven:

Diverse Approaches to *Dhikr*

The Moroccan tradition might emphasize rhythmic, communal *dhikr* with movement, while the Indo-Pakistani tradition might focus on silent meditation (*muraqaba*) on the Divine attributes. Turkish Sufis might incorporate music and poetry, while Gulf traditions might emphasize contemplative Qur'an recitation.

All these approaches are valid expressions of remembrance. As we recover, we might explore various traditions to find practices that resonate most deeply with our hearts.

Prayer Customs and Recovery Routines

Some cultures emphasize extended individual prayers after the obligatory *salah*; others focus on brief, consistent *wird* (litanies). Some traditions value dawn congregation prayers at the mosque; others prioritize nighttime devotions.

In recovery, we can adapt these cultural patterns to support our sobriety. What matters is consistency and sincerity, not adherence to one cultural expression over another.

Navigating Family Expectations

Cultural expectations around religious practice can sometimes create pressure that complicates recovery. Family members might expect certain outward expressions of devotion without understanding the inner work of recovery.

Finding the balance between honoring cultural traditions and developing an authentic personal practice is part of spiritual maturity in recovery.

Reflection Questions—Step Eleven

1. How has prayer or meditation helped me shift from self-will to spiritual alignment in daily life?

2. In what ways do I recognize Allah when I sit in silence or seek guidance?

3. What routines or distractions still prevent me from developing a deeper, conscious connection, and what can I do to create space for that relationship to grow?

The Wind Beneath Our Wings

We began this chapter with the image of wind: subtle, powerful, invisible, and transformative. This metaphor reflects the heart of Step Eleven. It represents our pursuit of a force we cannot see, yet one that reshapes every part of our lives.

Through prayer and meditation, we come to know this Divine Wind not only as an idea, but as a lived experience. We feel its movement. We respond to its currents. We place our trust in the direction it provides.

For Muslims in recovery, prayer and meditation are not optional practices. They are as essential as breath itself. These acts link us to our Creator, bring us back to our true selves, and connect us to the fellowship that supports our path.

The journey from addiction to spiritual awakening moves through many seasons. Sometimes the skies are clear and calm. Other times, we face storms and uncertainty. What grounds us is the rhythm of consistent return, meeting each day with intention, remembrance, and trust.

With every prayer, each moment of meditation, and every act of *dhikr*, we renew our commitment to Divine guidance. We turn toward illumination through surrender. We grow in clarity through remembering.

Step Eleven invites us to deepen. It draws us into a greater awareness of Allah and steadier alignment with His will. It teaches us to build a life anchored in presence, formed through practice, shaped by patience, and sustained by love.

As we move forward in recovery, may our hearts remain open to the gentle wind of Divine guidance. May we follow where it leads, confident in its wisdom. And in that unseen movement, may we come to know the nearness of Allah, always guiding us toward peace.

Chapter Twelve

All Our Affairs

W e've come a long way from rock bottom and that first moment of surrender. The places where we once stood in pain, confusion, and uncertainty are now part of our story, no longer the lens through which we see ourselves. Step by step, we've moved through the path of recovery: admitting our powerlessness, coming to believe, surrendering our will, taking moral inventory, sharing our truths, becoming ready, humbly asking, making amends, and developing conscious contact with Allah.

Step Twelve marks a turning point. Here, recovery becomes a way of living. We serve others with the same compassion we once received. The light that helped us find our way now shines through us as a source of guidance for others.

Step Twelve contains three essential elements: experiencing a spiritual awakening, carrying the message to others, and practicing these principles in all our affairs. These actions form a life built on purpose, presence, and service.

Step 12: Having had a spiritual awakening as the result of these Steps, we tried to carry this message to alcoholics, and to practice these principles in all our affairs.

Big Book of Alcoholics Anonymous (4th Edition):

- "Helping others is the foundation stone of your recovery." -p. 97

- "Practical experience shows that nothing will so much insure immunity from drinking as intensive work with other alcoholics." - p. 89

Twelve Steps and Twelve Traditions:

- "A spiritual awakening, as the result of these Steps, means the newcomer has not only accepted a set of moral principles, but has become able to practice them." -p. 106

- "It is only at the end of the road that we realize how far we have come." -p. 107

- "Our Twelfth Step also says that as a result of practicing all the Steps, we have each found something called a spiritual awakening... most of our experiences are what the psychologist William James calls the 'educational variety'—gradual and cumulative." -p. 106-107

- "We must bring into all our relationships the same self-searching, honesty, humility, and concern for others that we bring to our A.A. group." -p. 112

Qur'anic Reference:

"And say, 'Indeed, my prayer, my sacrifice, my living and my dying are for Allah, Lord of the worlds." (Qur'an, 6:162)

Having Had a Spiritual Awakening

Let's be clear. This is the only step that unfolds naturally, in its own time, as the result of living the others with sincerity. You can't will yourself into a spiritual awakening. You can't fake it, manufacture it, or intellectualize your way into one. A spiritual awakening arrives by the will of Allah, in the time and manner He chooses.

It might come after two weeks of sobriety or after twenty years. It may arrive suddenly, like a bolt of lightning, or unfold slowly, like the first light of dawn. However it comes, it leaves no part of you unchanged.

> "Ideas, emotions, and attitudes which were once the guiding forces of the lives of these men are suddenly cast to one side, and a completely new set of conceptions and motives begins to dominate them."
>
> Alcoholics Anonymous p. 27

My awakening was subtle. So subtle, in fact, I didn't even realize it had happened until much later. The moment of realization came suddenly, but the awakening itself had been unfolding quietly beneath the surface. I can describe it in simple terms: I stopped calling my sponsor about sobriety-threatening issues and started calling about serenity-threatening ones.

In early recovery, everything felt like a threat to my sobriety. I was still obsessed. Still battling cravings. Still thinking about drinking, even when I was going through the motions; meetings, steps, prayer. But as I began to actually live the principles, something shifted. The obsession lifted. The cravings faded. And in their place came something else: peace. *Salaam.*

And then one day I looked up and realized: it's no longer my sobriety that's in danger—it's my serenity. The real threat wasn't alcohol anymore; it was distraction. *Dunya. Nafs.* The whisper of *waswās* hijacking my attention and pulling me out of presence. The real battlefield was my inner life.

> "It can come as a surprise to realize that treating yourself kindly and respectfully can feel like a spiritual experience, especially when you've spent years doing the opposite."

Anonymous

What I became conscious of wasn't just a new insight; it was the fact that I was spiritually awake. Not in some mystical, ego-gratifying way. Just aware. Tuned in. Heart-conscious more than mind-conscious. It wasn't about achieving something new, but about recognizing something ancient.

That is the nature of a true awakening.

The touch of the Divine reveals what has always been present. It uncovers rather than constructs, offering clarity rather than noise. What awakens in you was always there, waiting behind the noise. Like the sun behind the clouds. Like a diamond buried beneath years of rubble and regret.

That diamond is your *fitrah,* your original purity, the part of you that never left Allah, even when you thought you had.

And that light feeling? That's His love.

A love that has never, ever abandoned you. Not when you drank. Not when you relapsed. Not when you lied, stole, or sank. Allah's love didn't disappear. It simply waited. With patience. With mercy.

The awakening is not merely understanding this. It is feeling it in your bones. You will taste Mercy and know, with absolute certainty, that something always held you.

The Many Faces of Spiritual Awakening

The Big Book describes two types of spiritual awakening: the sudden, dramatic variety and the "educational variety" that happens gradually. In the Islamic tradition, we find similarly diverse experiences of spiritual illumination.

The Sudden Awakening: Lightning on the Path

Some experience a dramatic moment of clarity. What the Sufis call *jadhb* (divine attraction). Like Ibrahim, who, after hearing a soul-piercing voice, left his palace and wealth behind, or like the Prophet Muhammad (SAW), whose heart Jibril forever transformed the moment he revealed the Qur'an's first words in the Hira cave—these moments can instantly and completely reorient a life.

Signs of a sudden awakening may include:

- A profound sense of Divine presence

- Overwhelming emotion, often joy or tears

- A clear "before-and-after" feeling

- Immediate release from certain struggles

While these experiences are real, they aren't necessary for authentic spiritual transformation. The Prophet Muhammad (SAW) himself experienced both sudden revelations and gradual spiritual development over many years.

The Gradual Awakening: Dawn Breaking Slowly

More common is the gradual awakening, or what the 12 & 12 calls "educational variety." Like dawn breaking imperceptibly, we only realize the light has come when we look back and see how far we've traveled from the darkness.

Indicators of gradual awakening include:

- Noticing changed reactions to old triggers

- Feeling natural concern for others' welfare

- Finding that spiritual practices have become meaningful rather than mechanical

- Realizing that behaviors once impossible now come naturally

As Imam al-Ghazali's teachings suggest, the transformation of the heart is a gradual process, unfolding moment by moment.

Awakening Through Service: The Unexpected Gift

Many discover their spiritual awakening through acts of service. The paradox is clear: when we give; we receive. When we turn our attention outward, something within us changes.

This awakening reveals itself through:

- Finding joy in helping others without recognition

- Experiencing a sense of purpose in service

- Forgetting self-concern while focused on others' needs

- Discovering strength and wisdom you didn't know you had

Awakening Through Difficulty: The Blessing in Disguise

"Perhaps you hate a thing and it is good for you"

Qur'an, 2:216

Sometimes, spiritual awakening comes not through joyful revelation but through navigating hardship with faith.

This type of awakening is identifiable by:

- Finding peace amid circumstances that once would have destroyed you

- Experiencing gratitude, even during challenges

- Developing deeper compassion through your own suffering

- Seeing Divine wisdom in what once seemed senseless

"Sometimes Allah gives while depriving you, and sometimes He deprives you while giving to you."

Ibn 'Aṭā'illah al-Iskandarī, Kitab al-Ḥikam.

Some of the most profound awakenings arrive disguised as challenges. Difficulties in life, forcing complete reliance on our Higher Power, often bring about conditions preceding genuine spiritual growth. In active addiction, we become accustomed to running from our problems or using substances to dull them, rather than confronting and resolving them. As we say in recovery, "First it gets better, then it gets worse, then it gets real." Many people find their spiritual awakening right at the threshold of that last stage—when things get real. A crisis, a loss, or a deep internal reckoning becomes the catalyst that finally breaks their illusion of control and compels them to turn fully to Allah.

This is a gut check I have failed more than once on my journey. Before I came to Islam, I stayed sober for a couple of years, but I relapsed when I encountered a challenge for which I lacked spiritual preparation. The death of my mother was one such moment. I had not been working the Steps consistently, and when the grief came, I didn't have the foundation to withstand it. I turned to the bottle instead of turning to God. By the grace and mercy of Allah, I could bounce back. I eventually returned to the path and recommitted to my recovery.

I share this not to dramatize failure, but as a warning. You must rely on the tools we've built through the Steps, especially in the face of hardship. Remember by the time we reach Step 12 our lives are grounded in service to others. These tools are not just for early sobriety—they are the spiritual provisions that will sustain you through the long road ahead. Sobriety is a marathon, not a sprint. A spiritual awakening is a milestone on that journey, but it is not the destination. It marks the true beginning.

"Indeed, with hardship comes ease. Truly, with hardship comes ease."

Qur'an, 94:5–6

It's important to maintain perspective when we face life-altering challenges. In recovery, getting sober is only the beginning of a lifelong path. Notice that alcohol is only mentioned in Step One. As we continue working the Steps and deepening our spiritual growth, our lives expand—and that expansion brings both blessings and tests. The door to experience opens wider, and with it come both joy and difficulty.

Therefore *dhikr* is essential. *Alhamdulillāh* for the good times, and *alhamdulillāh* for the hard times—especially the hard times. The verse above reminds us ease always accompanies hardship. Training ourselves to be grateful for even hidden ease lightens the burden of hardship.

"This too shall pass"

As addicts, our default setting in difficulty is often to react without *adab*, and that reaction pulls us downward. When we sink, we risk relapse. But as we continue working the Steps and refining our hearts, we meet hard times with gratitude instead of panic. We remember that "this too shall pass," not as a cliché, but as a spiritual truth.

There is nothing in our lives—no hardship, no challenge, no grief, no test—that requires us to drink. There are no situations in which drinking will improve the outcome. Maintaining this clarity of perspective is essential. Every test is a chance to turn to Allah, to apply what we've learned, and to walk through difficulty with grace and presence.

The Essential Elements of All Awakenings

Whatever form it takes, authentic spiritual awakening in the Islamic tradition includes certain universal elements:

- Connection: A felt relationship with Allah, rather than just theoretical knowledge

- Transformation: Changed behavior flowing from a changed heart

- Service: Natural concern for others' well-being

- Perspective: Seeing this world in proper relation to the *akhirah* (hereafter)

- Presence: Increased awareness of the Divine in everyday life

The form your awakening takes matters less than its fruits.

> "The most beloved of people to Allah are those who are most beneficial to others."
>
> The Prophet Muhammad (SAW), Al-Mu'jam al-Awsat 5787

The measure of awakening lies in its expression. It shows in how we love, how we speak the truth, and how fully we show up. It reveals itself in sincere service, offered for the sake of Allah and the benefit of His creation.

For Those Still Waiting: When Awakening Seems Distant

Perhaps you've worked through the Steps sincerely but don't feel you've had a spiritual awakening. You may wonder: "Is something wrong with me? Have I missed a step? Will it ever happen?"

First, know that you're not alone. Many who later experienced profound awakening went through periods of what felt like spiritual dryness or disconnection. The great saints of Islam, including some companions of the Prophet (SAW), spoke of times when their hearts felt constricted rather than expanded.

> "The one who persists in knocking at the door will eventually enter."
>
> Imam Ali (ra), Nahj al-Balaghah, Hikmah 175

If you find yourself in this place, consider these perspectives:

You May Be More Awake Than You Realize

Often, we don't recognize our own spiritual growth because it happens so gradually. Like watching a child day by day, the changes can be imperceptible; then, someone who hasn't seen them for months exclaims at how much they've grown.

Ask yourself:

- Do I respond differently to challenges than I did before recovery?

- Has my perspective on life, purpose, and meaning shifted?

- Do I feel drawn to help others in ways I wouldn't have before?

- Have others commented on the changes they see in me?

These subtle shifts may be signs of an awakening you haven't yet recognized.

Expectation Can Block Experience

Sometimes our expectations about what a spiritual awakening "should" feel like prevent us from recognizing what's actually happening. We look for dramatic experiences and miss the quiet miracle unfolding within us. In Islam and in recovery, we focus more on intention rather than expectation. Expectations can lead to resentment.

The Sufis speak of "veiling through illumination," where our concept of spiritual experience actually becomes a veil that obscures our direct experience.

Try setting aside your expectations and simply being present to whatever is happening in your spiritual life right now, without judgment or comparison.

Trust the Process and Continue the Practice

If you don't feel spiritually awakened yet, the prescription is simple: continue the practices. Keep showing up. Keep working the Steps. Keep praying, even when it feels mechanical. Keep serving, even when you don't feel spiritually motivated.

The Islamic concept of *ihsan*—excellence in worship—doesn't depend on feelings. It's about consistent practice with the right intention, trusting that Allah sees what we cannot yet see.

Consider Working with a Guide

Sometimes we need someone with more experience to help us recognize our spiritual progress or to identify what might block our awareness. This could be a sponsor, a spiritual director, an imam, or someone else with wisdom in both recovery and spiritual matters.

> *"No one humbles himself for the sake of Allah except that Allah raises him."*
> Prophet Muhammad (SAW), Sahih Muslim 2588

The very act of seeking guidance shows the humility that opens the door to spiritual growth.

Awakening Is a Gift, Not an Achievement

Finally, remember that no one can force or earn spiritual awakening. It is a gift from Allah, given according to His wisdom and timing. Our responsibility is simply to create the conditions where it can occur; through prayer, service, honest self-examination, and persistent practice of spiritual principles.

> *"Allah knows, while you do not know"*
> Qur'an, 2:216

Trust in divine timing and continue. The dawn may be closer than you think.

Qur'anic and Prophetic Witness to Awakening

The spiritual awakening described in Step Twelve is known in the Islamic tradition by many names: *tawba nasuh* (a sincere turning), *basirah* (inner sight), *yaqin* (certainty), and ultimately *ma'rifah*—a deep, experiential knowing of Allah.

This is the moment the heart wakes up with full presence.

> *"Is one whose heart Allah has opened to Islam, so that he has received a light from his Lord, [like one who is still in darkness]?"*
>
> Qur'an, 39:22

Here, the description of awakening is the heart opening and receiving *nur min rabbihi*, a light from its Lord. That is the light we feel in Step Twelve. Not something we generate, but something gifted. A Divine spark that sets the soul aflame.

> *"And thus We have revealed to you an inspiration of Our command. You knew not what the Book was, nor what faith was. But We have made it a light by which We guide whom We will of Our servants."*
>
> Qur'an, 42:52

The light of Allah is a real and active force, not a symbol. Only through being guided by this light does a person become ready to guide others.

> *"Beware. There is a piece of flesh in the body—if it is sound, the whole body is sound; and if it is corrupt, the whole body is corrupt. That piece is the heart."*
>
> The Prophet Muhammad (SAW), Sahih al-Bukhari 52

A spiritual awakening is the purification of the heart. It is when the *qalb* becomes soft, receptive to Divine truth. It's when we stop being ruled by the ego and start being guided by the heart.

"Indeed, those who have said, 'Our Lord is Allah' and then remained steadfast—the angels descend upon them, [saying], 'Do not fear and do not grieve but receive good tidings of Paradise, which you were promised."

Qur'an, 41:30

Those who have turned, surrendered, and remained steadfast; they are granted *tama'ninah* (tranquility), *mahabba* (love), and, ultimately, a glimpse of the nearness of Allah in this life.

The Self Cannot Carry the Light

The great Sufi teachers knew this well. They taught that you cannot reach true Divine proximity while clinging to the illusion of a separate self.

> "You only know the universe according to the amount you know the shadows, and you are ignorant of the Real according to what you do not know of the person on which that shadow depends."
>
> Ibn 'Arabi, The Bezels of Wisdom

True service means dissolving the illusion that you are the doer. True love means removing yourself from the center. True light only shines when the ego steps aside.

Therefore, Step Twelve is not a command; it's a result. It says, "Having had a spiritual awakening..." not "Create one." It reminds us: You don't awaken yourself. Allah awakens you.

Only then are you ready to serve, guided by Spirit rather than self.

Carry This Message

Once this experience takes place and your inner lamp is lit, a responsibility arises. You must carry this message to others. That's not optional. It's a trust. A sacred *amanah*.

"Every soul is responsible for what it has earned."

Qur'an, 74:38

Islam emphasizes personal responsibility. You must walk your path. No one can repent for you. No one can believe for you. No one can surrender for you.

Likewise, no one can work your steps. No one can recover for you.

However, once Allah has blessed you with an awakening, you become a carrier of light. Your very being becomes a message. It is a calling to serve.

You sit with the newcomer. You pick up the phone. You listen. You pray. You show up. Divine Light has touched you.

And a light, once lit, must shine.

Give it away to keep it

There's an important relationship between spiritual awakening and service that's easy to miss. While Step Twelve presents them sequentially, first awakening, then service. The reality is more cyclical:

- Awakening enables service: The spiritual connection we develop gives us the strength, clarity, and compassion to help others effectively.

- Service deepens awakening: When we help others, our own connection with Allah often intensifies in unexpected ways.

This creates a virtuous cycle. Our initial awakening, however small, enables us to serve others. That service then deepens and expands our spiritual awakening, which enhances our capacity for service. And so it continues, with each element reinforcing the other.

The Prophet Muhammad (SAW) demonstrated this perfectly. His initial spiritual experiences in the Cave of Hira prepared him for his mission of service. Then, through his years of serving humanity, his spiritual connection continued to deepen and develop.

"Whoever relieves a believer's distress in this world, Allah will relieve his distress on the Day of Resurrection."

Prophet Muhammad (SAW), Sahih Muslim 2699

In recovery terms, this means we don't need to wait for a "complete" spiritual awakening before beginning to help others. Even a glimmer of light is enough to start. And as we share that light, it grows brighter within us.

This understanding helps us avoid two common pitfalls:

1. Waiting for a "perfect" awakening before beginning to serve

2. Burning out in service because we've neglected our spiritual connection

The balanced approach is constant movement between inner development and outer service. Drawing from the well of Allah's mercy, then sharing that water with others, then returning to the well for replenishment, in an endless cycle of receiving and giving.

Many paraphrase Ibn Ata'illah: "Gratitude seeds the tree of service, which the rain of remembrance waters."

Carrying the Message: A Sacred Art

Carrying the message is both a privilege and a responsibility. But how do we do this effectively, without falling into the traps of ego, preaching, or imposing our journey on others? Here are some practical principles drawn from both recovery wisdom and Islamic spiritual tradition.

Attraction Rather Than Promotion

The most powerful message is a life transformed. As the Prophet Muhammad (SAW) taught through his example, our actions speak louder than our words. Authentic change draws people in, unlike empty claims or zealous recruitment.

This means:

- Letting your serenity, joy, and stability be visible without boasting

- Sharing your experience when asked, rather than forcing it on others

- Living the principles openly without claiming spiritual superiority

Meet People Where They Are

The Prophet's (SAW) ability to speak to each person according to their understanding was widely recognized. Similarly, effective twelfth-step work means adapting our approach to the individual before us.

This involves:

- Listening first, speaking second

- Using language the person can relate to

- Respecting where they are in their journey, not where you think they should be

Share Experience, Not Theory

We transmit recovery through sincere connection. What touches hearts is not your accumulated knowledge, but your lived experience.

Remember to:

- Share what happened, what changed, and what it's like now

- Be honest about your struggles, not just your successes

- Focus on feelings and experiences rather than abstract concepts

Maintain Appropriate Boundaries

Service without boundaries can become harmful to both parties. Islamic tradition emphasizes the right relationship in all matters.

This means:

- Recognizing the limits of your role and expertise.

- Knowing when to refer someone for professional help.

- Taking care of your own recovery so you remain effective in service.

- Never exploit those you help for emotional, financial, or other gain.

Respect Divine Timing

We cannot force awakening in another person.

"Indeed, you do not guide whom you like, but Allah guides whom He wills. And He is most knowing of the [rightly] guided."

Qur'an, 28:56

This requires:

- Patience with those who aren't ready

- Letting go of results and expectations

- Trusting that Allah works in each person's life according to Divine wisdom

Remember It's Not About You

Perhaps the most important principle: when carrying the message, we are channels, not sources. The healing comes from Allah, not from us.

This perspective helps us:

- Remain humble in your service.

- Avoid taking credit for others' recovery.

- Stay focused on the message rather than our messenger.

When we approach carrying the message with these principles, we fulfill our responsibility while honoring both the dignity of those we serve and the Divine source of all healing. We serve not as preachers or saviors, but as witnesses, testifying to what Allah has done in our lives and what He can do in theirs.

Building Recovery Resources in the Muslim Community

As Muslims in recovery, we carry a dual responsibility: to support fellow recovering addicts and to help develop resources for recovery within our own Muslim communities. The stigma around addiction in many Muslim communities limits or eliminates culturally sensitive recovery support.

Some practical ways to fulfill this responsibility include:

- Working with imams and community leaders to increase understanding of addiction as a disease, not just a moral failing

- Helping to establish *halaqas* (study circles) specifically for Muslims in recovery

- Mentoring other Muslims in recovery, especially those early in their journey

- Creating literature and resources that address the unique needs of Muslims in recovery

- Organizing sober social gatherings for Muslims who need alcohol-free environments

By building these resources, we make contributions. We create pathways for those who will come after us, making their journey of recovery a little easier because of our service.

Navigating Muslim-Specific Recovery Challenges

Carrying the message effectively within Muslim communities requires understanding the unique challenges many Muslims face in recovery.

Cultural and Family Expectations

Many Muslim families struggle to acknowledge addiction openly, viewing it as bringing shame to the family. This can make it difficult for individuals to seek help or to speak honestly about their recovery journey.

When carrying the message, be sensitive to these dynamics. Help newcomers navigate family conversations about recovery and find language that honors their culture while maintaining their recovery needs.

Social Gatherings and Religious Celebrations

Weddings and other cultural celebrations can be challenging for Muslims in recovery, especially when alcohol is present or when cultural norms promote drinking despite Islamic teachings.

Here are a few practical strategies for navigating these situations, such as bringing your own beverages, attending with a sober friend, planning your exit in advance, or parking on the street to avoid being blocked in. Organizing alternative gatherings or creating sober Muslim social events can offer meaningful support and connection.

Reconciling Religious Identity with Recovery Identity

Some Muslims in recovery struggle to integrate their Muslim identity with their recovery program, especially if they're attending secular recovery meetings or have drifted from Islamic practice during active addiction.

Help them see that authentic recovery and authentic faith are complementary, not competitive. The principles of the recovery program align beautifully with Islamic values, and each can strengthen the other.

Finding Culturally Sensitive Professional Help

Finding professionals who understand both addiction and Muslim cultural contexts is challenging when additional mental health or trauma support is needed.

Develop a resource list of culturally sensitive providers and advocate for increased cultural competence in treatment settings. Sometimes, being the bridge between these worlds is, in itself, a form of carrying the message.

By addressing these specific challenges, we make the recovery path more accessible to fellow Muslims, fulfilling our responsibility to carry the message in the most effective way possible.

Beyond the Rooms: A Life of Service

Step Twelve tells us to carry the message to other alcoholics. And that is holy work—no question. It's what kept us alive in our earliest days of recovery. It's how we repay the debt we owe to those who have helped us.

> "*Ihsān* is not only worshiping with awareness, but acting with excellence in all things—especially in service, for that is where the heart's sincerity is tested."
>
> Ibn Qayyim al-Jawziyya, Madarij al-Salikin

There is an entire world beyond the rooms. There are people who will never sit in a circle of chairs, but are drowning just the same. Addicted to status. Consumed by anger. Distracted by sin. Lost in *dunya*.

We are called be an example to everyone, regardless of station.

The promise of Step Twelve is that we no longer live for ourselves alone. Recovery isn't just sobriety—it's the restoration of responsibility. Of presence. Of purpose.

> "A kindly act once in a while isn't enough. You have to act the Good Samaritan every day, if need be."
>
> Alcoholics Anonymous, p. 97

And that purpose is service. Not just for alcoholics. Not just for addicts.
But to all of humanity.

Islam: A Religion of Sacred Service

> *"And they give food in spite of love for it to the needy, the orphan, and the captive, [saying], 'We feed you only for the countenance of Allah. We wish not from you reward or gratitude."*
>
> Qur'an, 76:8-9

We give true service for the sake of Allah, not for thanks, applause, or recognition. It's quiet. Sincere. Done, even when no one is watching.

> *"The best of people are those who are most beneficial to others."*
> Prophet Muhammad (SAW), al-Muʿjam al-Awsaṭ

This is an explicit instruction. Your value is not measured by your bank account, your sobriety coins, or how long you've been clean. Instead, it is measured by your usefulness, your good deeds and your love in action.

"Worship Allah and associate nothing with Him, and to parents do good, and to relatives, orphans, the needy, the near neighbor, the neighbor farther away, the companion at your side, the traveler, and those whom your right hands possess. Indeed, Allah does not like those who are self-deluding and b oastful."

Qur'an, 4:36

Service in Islam flows outward in every direction. It includes parents, neighbors, strangers, those near and far, even travelers, and animals. True service grows from a heart aligned with sincerity. It begins when the *nafs* moves aside, and the soul steps forward. The fruit of awakening appears in this posture of service, not in fleeting emotional highs or dramatic moments.

When Allah grants you awakening, He is also entrusting you with a message. And that message must be lived. Not just spoken. Not just quoted. Lived.

You carry it into your marriage. Into traffic. Into work. Into the grocery store.

You carry it when no one sees. You carry it when it's hard. You carry it when your ego wants to fight and you choose peace instead.

Islam makes it clear: every action matters. Every choice echoes in eternity.

"Whoever removes a hardship from a believer in this world, Allah will remove one of his hardships on the Day of Judgment."
Prophet Muhammad (SAW), Sahih Muslim 2699

So, by all means, carry the message and don't stop at the meeting room door.

Carry it into the world.

Because the light Allah gave you is meant to shine everywhere.

Practice These Principles in All Our Affairs

This is the culminating message of the Steps. The final ripple that touches every shore of our lives:

"Practice these principles in all our affairs."

Not some. Not most. All.

Here is where recovery becomes life. Where the steps are no longer something we do, but something we are. It's the embodiment of transformation. At the dinner table. At work. In solitude. Online. With strangers. With loved ones. With enemies. Everywhere.

And in the Islamic tradition, this level of presence has a name: *Adab*.

Adab: The Art of Being in Harmony with the Divine

Remember, *adab* is beyond just manners. It's the spiritual etiquette of the heart. It's behaving as if Allah is watching, because He is. This is the fruit of a heart that humility, awakening, and a return to its Source have produced.

As commonly expressed in Islamic spiritual teachings: "The one who has *adab* with Allah has *adab* with creation." This principle echoes the writings of scholars such as Imam al-Ghazali and Shaykh Ibn 'Ajiba, who describe *adab* as both a vertical relationship with the Divine and a horizontal relationship with others.

A person who has truly walked the path cannot compartmentalize their righteousness. It flows through everything. They understand that each moment is sacred, each action is recorded, and each interaction offers an opportunity to reflect the Light of The One who awakened them.

This is what it means to "practice the principles in all our affairs." It is to live with *taqwa* (God-consciousness), *rahma* (mercy), *sidq* (truthfulness), and *sabr* (patience) not just when it's easy—but when no one sees. When your ego screams. When life feels unfair.

> *"Indeed, the most noble of you in the sight of Allah is the most righteous of you."*
>
> Qur'an, 49:13

All Our Affairs: From Recovery to Life

This last instruction of Step Twelve is perhaps its most far-reaching. But what does this look like in practical terms across the various domains of life?

In Family Relationships

The principles of honesty, humility, and making amends transform how we show up as parents, children, siblings, and spouses.

This means:

- Being present and attentive, not just physically but emotionally

- Admitting when we're wrong, even to our children

- Setting healthy boundaries while maintaining compassion

- Prioritizing relationships over being "right"

As the Prophet (SAW) said: *"The best of you are those who are best to their families."* Our recovery is measured not by spiritual experiences, but by how we treat those closest to us.

In Work and Financial Affairs

Recovery principles apply no less to our professional lives and financial dealings.

This looks like:

- Bringing integrity to every transaction

- Treating colleagues and customers with respect

- Working for excellence rather than praise

- Managing money with balance, neither hoarding nor being wasteful

The Islamic concept of *barakah* (divine blessing) reminds us that honest work and fair dealings invite Allah's blessing, regardless of the amount of profit.

In Community and Citizenship

Our recovery extends into how we take part in our broader communities, both Muslim and societal.

Recovery principles guide us to:

- Contribute positively to community well-being

- Stay informed and engaged in civic matters

- Approach political differences with respect and open-mindedness

- Use our voice and vote to uphold justice and compassion

"O you who believe, be persistently standing firm in justice, witnesses for Allah, even if it be against yourselves or parents and relatives"

Qur'an, 4:135

In Times of Difficulty and Loss

Recovery principles are perhaps most tested, and most valuable, during life's inevitable hardships.

In these times, we practice:

- Acceptance without resignation

- Patience without passivity

- Trust in Divine wisdom while taking appropriate action

- Reaching out for support rather than isolating

The Islamic concept of *sabr* (patient perseverance) teaches us that enduring hardship with consciousness of Allah transforms difficulty into spiritual growth.

In Moments of Joy and Success

Surprisingly, many find that practicing principles during success is harder than during struggle.

This requires:

- Maintaining gratitude rather than entitlement

- Sharing blessings rather than hoarding them

- Remembering Allah in prosperity, not just in need

- Staying connected to the community rather than elevating above it

"No! [But] indeed, man transgresses because he sees himself self-sufficient"
Qur'an 96:6-7

In Spiritual Practice

Even our religious observance benefits from recovery principles.

This means approaching worship with:

- Humility rather than spiritual pride

- Consistency rather than dramatic intensity

- Balance between ritual and inner meaning

- Community connection rather than isolated piety

"The most beloved deeds to Allah are those that are consistent, even if they are small."
Prophet Muhammad (SAW), Sahih al-Bukhari 6465; Sahih Muslim 783

Practicing principles in all our affairs reflects conscious intention, sincere effort, and a willingness to return to the path when we drift. It allows the transformation that began in recovery to reach every part of our lives, steadily and patiently, with persistence, until our life itself becomes a witness to the healing power of these spiritual principles.

Practical Challenges: When Principle Meets Reality

Applying spiritual principles in everyday life often presents specific challenges. Here are some common situations Muslims in recovery face, and approaches for navigating them while maintaining spiritual integrity:

During Ramadan and Other Religious Observances

Ramadan and other spiritual seasons can be both strengthening and challenging for those in recovery. The increased spiritual focus offers support, but changes in routine, family gatherings, and potential triggers require careful navigation.

Practical approaches include:

- Maintaining regular contact with recovery support during religious holidays

- Planning ahead for family gatherings where triggers might be present

- Adjusting meeting schedules rather than eliminating them during Ramadan

- Seeing fasting as an opportunity to deepen the spiritual principles of recovery

At Cultural Celebrations and Weddings

Weddings and celebrations can present challenges when cultural practices around hospitality sometimes conflict with recovery needs.

Strategies include:

- Arriving early and connecting with the servers about non-alcoholic options

- Bringing a sober companion when possible

- Having prepared responses for offers of drinks

- Planning an exit strategy if the environment becomes threatening to sobriety

In Business and Professional Settings

Business environments often present unique challenges, especially when client meetings or networking events center on alcohol.

Practical approaches include:

- Suggesting coffee meetings instead of happy hours

- Arriving at functions early and establishing yourself with a non-alcoholic beverage

- Developing comfort with simply saying "I don't drink" without elaborate explanations

- Finding Muslim business networks where shared values support recovery

From Powerlessness to Purified Action

Remember where you started.

We began this journey at rock bottom. Lost in self. Shattered by ego. Spiritually bankrupt.

And now, by the grace of Allah, we are called to reflect His mercy in action.

To let the awakened heart move the hands. To live what we know. To be the message. This is not a call to perfection. It is a call to progress. To presence. To *Ihsan*.

> "*My servant does not draw near to Me with anything more beloved to Me than the religious duties I have imposed upon him. And My servant continues to draw near to Me with supererogatory works until I love him. When I love him, I become his hearing with which he hears, his seeing with which he sees, his hand with which he strikes, and his foot with which he walks. Were he to ask of Me, I would surely give him; and were he to seek refuge in Me, I would surely protect him.*"
> Prophet Muhammad (SAW), Book of Softening the Hearts , Book 76:,
> Hadith 6502

Step Twelve essentially means living with the awareness that someone witnesses every moment, every action is significant, and every choice is a spiritual decision. Not out of fear, but out of love. Not out of obligation, but out of awakening.

Following the Twelve Steps has brought us home, not by taking us somewhere new, but by returning us to our souls' rightful place. We have moved from the chaos of addiction to the peace of surrender, from the isolation of self-will to the connection found in divine guidance, from liquor to *dhikr*, from substance to essence.

Reflection Questions

How does the Islamic concept of *ihsān* deepen your understanding of carrying the message to others with sincerity and excellence?

In what ways can acts of service be a form of worship (*ʿibādah*) in your daily life?

The Prophet (SAW) said, "*None of you truly believes until he loves for his brother what he loves for himself.*" How can this teaching guide your approach to helping others in recovery?

Reflection

"Allah does not look at your outward forms or your wealth, but He looks at your hearts and your deeds."

The Prophet Muhammad (SAW)

With that teaching in mind, everything in this book—everything in recovery, and everything in Islam—leads back to a single question: Have you surrendered?

We begin surrender in Step One, when we admit that our lives have become unmanageable and that we are powerless over alcohol. In Step Two, we surrender our prejudices by opening the door to the possibility of God. In Step Three, we surrender our will by deciding to let God guide us. In Steps Four and Five, we surrender our pride by writing a moral inventory and sharing the wreckage of our past. In Steps Six and Seven, we surrender our character defects, many of which have formed the foundation of our identity. In Steps Eight and Nine, we surrender who we used to be by taking full responsibility and making amends. Through living amends, we step into our purified hearts. In Step Ten, we surrender our complacency by maintaining a daily spiritual practice and promptly admitting our faults. In Step Eleven, we surrender our desires by praying only for knowledge of God's will and for the power to carry it out. And in Step Twelve, we surrender ourselves completely by living in service and carrying the message to others.

Step Twelve reflects the surrender that begins in Step One. Our illness stems from selfishness and self-centeredness. By the time we reach the last step, we are no longer focused on ourselves. We have turned our attention to the well-being of others.

"None of you truly believes until he loves for his brother what he loves for himself."

The Prophet Muhammad (SAW)

There are people in recovery meetings, detox centers, halfway houses, and quiet places around the world who are walking this same path. They may not use the word *Allah*. They may not have heard the word *Islam*. But if they have made the Third Step decision—if they have turned their will and their life over to the care of the God of their understanding—then they have surrendered. In that moment, they are living in alignment with the essence of Islam, even if they have never called it that.

The word *Islam* means surrender, and that surrender begins in the heart. It is not a label or a category. We cannot see it from the outside or measure it by the names we give ourselves. It begins the moment you place your trust in the unseen and allow your heart to be led by something greater than your own will. It deepens through honesty, remembrance, and the willingness to let go of control. This is the path of the seeker. This is the return to *fitrah*—the original purity placed in every soul by its Creator.

What matters is the connection between the heart and the Creator. The heart is a mirror, designed to reflect the truth it was created to know. When we begin to surrender, that mirror clears. As we continue in honesty and remembrance, what we reflect becomes more accurate. Through this reflection, we recognize our place in creation and the nearness of The One who crafted us.

"The eye through which I see God is the same eye through which God sees me."

Ibn 'Arabī

To connect with the God of your understanding is to allow yourself to be known and to know. It is not about defining God with precision. It is about showing up honestly, placing your trust in the care of the Creator, and allowing your life to become a reflection of that trust.

This is not a matter of creed or conversion. It is a matter of sincerity. Allah knows what lives in every heart. The Qur'an affirms this clearly:

"Indeed, those who believe, and those who are Jews, and the Sabeans, and the Christians, and the Magians, and those who associate others with Allah—Allah will judge between them on the Day of Resurrection. Indeed, Allah is Witness over all things."

Qur'an, 22:17

This verse tells us something essential. No one finds salvation through a label. Labels do not cast anyone away. What matters is the heart's condition and the choices a soul makes. What matters is sincerity, humility, and the desire to walk in the light of truth.

The purpose of this book is not to offer a new religion or a revised program. Its purpose is to show that the path of recovery and the path of Islam follow the same map. Both begin with the admission of powerlessness. Both deepen through trust in The One who holds all power. Both unfold through remembrance, self-examination, service, and surrender.

There is no need to change religions in order to walk this path. Our only requirement was a desire to stop drinking. There is no requirement to speak in a specific language or adopt a particular form. What matters is whether you speak from the heart.

So call. And keep calling. With your breath, with your heart. A heart purified through the mercy of Allah will guide you as you journey forth on road of happy destiny.

"Call upon Me, and I will respond to you."

Qur'an, 40:60

On Fellowship

From the beginning, AA made it clear: you will not recover alone. This isn't just a suggestion. It's structural. The program builds around "we," not "me," including meetings, sponsorship, group conscience, and literature.

> "The feeling of having shared in a common peril is one element in the powerful cement which binds us. But that in itself would never have held us together as we are now joined."
>
> Alcoholics Anonymous, p. 17

In recovery, it's not enough to believe. Wanting it is insufficient. Do it. Work to **stay connected**. Call your sponsor. Go to the meetings. Show up. Listen. Share. Cry. Laugh. Keep your seat warm so someone else can find theirs.

The disease wants you alone. The solution demands that you return to the circle.

> *"Hold firmly to the rope of Allah all together and do not become divided. And remember the favor of Allah upon you---when you were enemies and He brought your hearts together and you became, by His favor, brothers."*
>
> Qur'an, 3:103

This verse reveals the essence of fellowship: shared guidance, mutual support, and hearts brought to wholeness through unity under Divine will. The purpose is not comfort, but transformation through connection. Islam affirms community as essential for spiritual survival.

The Path of *Suhba*

In the Islamic tradition, spiritual transformation is never a solo journey.

The Prophet's (SAW) mission, from the earliest days of the *ummah*, was to a community, not to an individual. He did not have disciples; he had companions. They served as mirrors, shoulders, correctives, and protectors for one another. The religion spread not only through *da'wah* but through companionship, through *suhba*.

> "The believer is to the believer like a solid structure, each part supporting the other."
>
> Prophet Muhammad (SAW), Sahih al-Bukhari 481

In recovery, as in Islam, a strong support network is essential. You need people in your corner. People who will answer the phone at 3 a.m. when your mind feeds you lies. People who will sit with you when you are unraveling. Who will remind you that you are not alone, that you matter, and that mercy is always near? Whether it is your sponsor, your home group, your brothers or sisters at the *masjid*, or that one friend who always tells you the truth, fellowship acts as spiritual armor. It helps keep you anchored in reality when the disease tries to pull you into despair.

> "The wolf devours the lone sheep."
>
> Prophet Muhammad (SAW), Sunan Abu Dawood 547

That is why we should remember to pick up the phone before picking up the bottle. We build recovery through connection. And connection saves lives.

We are created to walk together to be together. That design reflects Divine wisdom.

> *"And keep yourself patiently with those who call on their Lord morning and evening, seeking His Face; and do not let your eyes pass beyond them..."*
>
> Qur'an, 18:28

This verse offers more than a reminder about humility; it gives a prescription for *suhba*. Stay close to those who remember Allah. Gravitate toward those who bring you back to

Him. Let your soul choose connection over isolation and seek the company that nourishes your heart.

Suhba in Islmaic Spirituality

In the Sufi path, *suhba* is much more than a casual friendship. It's spiritual companionship. It's the lifeline that keeps the seeker grounded, accountable, and honest. *Suhba* allows the passing of spiritual states, the softening of hearts, and the seeing and healing of shadows in another's presence.

> "If you cannot find a perfect guide, then find righteous company. The companionship of the sincere is a mirror that reveals your state."
>
> Imam al-Qushayri, Risalah al-Qushayriyyah

The Sufis say that a single moment of true *suhba,* sitting sincerely with someone who remembers Allah, can do what years of isolated worship cannot.

This teaching reflects spiritual reality. Transformation begins with reflection, and reflection takes shape in the presence of others.

Suhba in Recovery

This is the purpose of fellowship. This is the role of the home group. Isolation creates vulnerability: to relapse, to self-deception, to spiritual inflation. It makes it easier to forget where we came from and where we are going.

In both Islam and recovery, the truth is the same: you cannot heal alone.

> "We are like the passengers of a great liner the moment after rescue from shipwreck. When camaraderie, joyousness and democracy pervade the vessel from steerage to Captain's table. Unlike the feelings of the ship's passengers, however, our joy in escape from disaster does not subside as we go our individual ways. The feeling of having shared in a common peril is one element in the powerful cement which binds us."
>
> Alcoholics Anonymous p. 17

You need people who remind you of who you were. Who hold you accountable to who you're becoming. Who pray for you when you're too tired to pray for yourself. Who remind you through their presence, their honesty, their stability: that Allah is near.

This is *suhba*.

And without it, we fall back into self-reliance. We drift toward ego. We lose the tether. And the wolf is waiting.

The Sponsor as a Spiritual Guide

When I think about my sponsor, I think of *suhba* in action. He's not a Muslim. He's never quoted Qur'an to me. But he has something that matters even more: presence. He listens. He shows up. He tells me the truth when I don't want to hear it. Especially when I don't want to hear it. That's what a proper guide does. They love you enough to be honest with you.

In the Sufi tradition, the *Shaikh* serves a similar role. Not to control or command, but to reflect. To correct. To guide your path with more clarity and experience. A real sponsor, like a real *shaikh*, doesn't tell you what you want to hear---they tell you what you *need* to hear. And if you're lucky, they'll do it with enough gentleness to keep you from running, and enough firmness to keep you from lying to yourself. Ultimately, a sponsor will hold you spiritually accountable.

What Happens if I disconnect?

I've fallen away from meetings before. Every time I thought I was too busy, too tired, too "okay," it started the same way: I let the *dunya* pull at my schedule. I let my *nafs* tell me I didn't need to go. That I've heard it all before. That I had a handle on things now.

But missing meetings meant missing connection. And missing connection meant losing accountability. And once I stopped being accountable to others, it wasn't long before I stopped being accountable to myself.

That's how "dry drunk" becomes *drunk drunk*.

Recovery is more than abstaining from alcohol; it is about staying in the flow of truth. For me, that means I need the rooms. I need the people. I need to remember where I come from. Hearing someone's Day One reminds me of the foundation of my Day 1,826. I need to share so my voice doesn't distort the truth.

Because when I'm not tending to my recovery, my disease is tending to me.

Zealots and Noise

Like any institution, AA has its extremists. So does the *Ummah*. So does every religious, political, or spiritual system ever created. You'll find people who are maximizers and extremists. People who police tone and posture. People who mistake certainty for wisdom.

But here's the truth: I don't engage with any of that.

The only "all or none" that matters to me is this: *Am I serving Allah, or am I serving myself?*

That's it.

I don't let someone else's attitude or opinion derail me from the path. When someone's judgment gets under my skin, I ask myself one simple question:

> "What does this have to do with my decision to stay sober today?"
> The answer is always the same: **Nothing**.

So, I stay in my lane. I mind my side of the street. I listen. I serve. I keep showing up. And I let Allah sort the rest.

The Lord's Prayer Dilemma

In many 12-step groups around the world, it is common to close the meeting with a prayer. So, from your very first AA meeting, you're likely to encounter the Lord's Prayer. As the meeting concludes, participants often stand, join hands, and recite this prayer together. For many Muslims, especially those new to the faith or in early recovery, this moment can evoke a mix of emotions: respect for the shared journey, yet uncertainty about participating in a prayer that doesn't align with Islamic teachings.

Islam emphasizes the oneness of God (*tawḥīd*) and cautions against associating partners with Him. The term "Father" used in the Lord's Prayer is a theological concept that doesn't align with Islamic monotheism.

> "A key difference is that the Lord's Prayer begins with 'Our Father,' whereas *Surah Al-Fatiha* refers to God as 'Rabb' (Lord), aligning with Islamic theology."

Dr. Shabir Ally

In navigating this, many Muslims choose to stand respectfully during the recitation, joining hands as a sign of unity, but silently reciting a personal supplication or remembrance (dhikr) that aligns with Islamic beliefs. This approach maintains the spirit of fellowship and mutual respect without compromising one's faith.

Personally, during this moment, I quietly say "Ya Allah" instead of "Our Father." This practice allows me to take part in the communal aspect of the meeting while staying true to my faith. It's a personal choice that reflects my intention to honor both my commitment to Islam and the shared journey of recovery.

It's essential to approach this with both sincerity and knowledge. If uncertain, consulting a knowledgeable scholar can provide guidance tailored to individual circumstances. The key is to uphold the principles of Islam while honoring the shared commitment to recovery.

Navigating Gender Interaction in Recovery Meetings

For many Muslims, the concept of *ikhtilāṭ* (the intermingling of men and women) raises valid concerns, particularly in settings like recovery meetings where such interactions are common. Islam places a strong emphasis on modesty and boundaries between genders to prevent any form of impropriety.

> *"And when you ask [his wives] for something, ask them from behind a partition. That is purer for your hearts and their hearts."*
>
> Qur'an, 33:53

This verse underscores the importance of maintaining respectful boundaries to safeguard the hearts and intentions of all individuals.

In recovery, it's essential to balance these principles with the necessity of seeking help and support. Many recovery programs, including Alcoholics Anonymous (AA), offer gender-specific meetings, such as men's or women's meetings, which can provide a more comfortable environment for those concerned about mixed-gender settings. These meetings address specific needs and can be a valuable resource.

However, in situations where only mixed-gender meetings are available, it's important to remember that the primary goal is healing and recovery. Islam recognizes the importance of intention (*niyyah*) in all actions. If someone intends to seek help and maintain sobriety, they may permissibly attend such meetings, provided they observe Islamic guidelines on modesty and interaction.

As always, consulting with a knowledgeable scholar can provide personalized guidance based on individual circumstances. The path to recovery is a journey, and Islam encourages seeking the means necessary to preserve one's health and well-being.

Fellowship as Spiritual Medicine

The disease of addiction is cunning, baffling, and powerful. One of its favorite tactics is isolation.

When we're alone, our thoughts don't have to answer to anyone. Our thoughts get louder. Our *nafs* gets comfortable. Resentments start to fester. Self-pity creeps back in. And before we know it, we're right back where we started. Not quite with a drink in hand just yet, but with a hardened heart, a restless soul, and a spiritual condition that's slipping through our fingers.

> "When you're alone with your thoughts, you're in a dangerous neighborhood."

Fellowship is the treatment.

In AA, we don't just go to meetings for accountability. We go because hearing someone else's story re-calibrates our own. We go because when someone shares their struggle out loud, it often unmasks the exact thing we were trying to hide. We go because someone's Day One reminds us that our Day One wasn't that long ago and could come again tomorrow if we're not vigilant.

In Islam, the same principle applies. Allah tells us:

> *"And remind, for indeed, the reminder benefits the believers."*
>
> Qur'an, 51:55

Reminders only work if there's someone around to remind you.

Remember, it's more than about being helped. It's about being helpful. In both Islam and recovery, service is medicine. Healing.

Helping others helps us. Carrying the message is how we stay spiritually awake. Showing up for someone else is often what keeps us from falling asleep at the wheel of our own recovery.

We get sick alone. We get well together.

You don't need to have all the answers. You don't need to be perfect. You just need to stay in the circle. Stay reachable. Stay honest.

That's the miracle of fellowship.

Dhikr

*W*hat is Dhikr? Dhikr, means "remembrance," is the spiritual practice of consciously recalling and praising Allah—through spoken words, silent reflection, or inner awareness. In Islamic tradition, dhikr is to the heart what water is to a plant: it nourishes, revives, and sustains the soul.

For those in recovery, dhikr aligns closely with Step Eleven's invitation to deepen "prayer and meditation to improve our conscious contact with God." It helps quiet the mind, center the heart, and reconnect us to our source of strength and guidance.

Dhikr is not merely repetition—it is an intentional act of turning the heart toward Allah, grounding us in presence, humility, and divine awareness. It serves as both a shield against distraction and a lifeline back to spiritual clarity.

Common Forms of Dhikr: These phrases can be repeated quietly, aloud, or even silently throughout the day:

Subḥānallāh

- Meaning: "Glory be to Allah" or "Exalted is God"

- Use: Expressing awe, humility, or recognizing the perfection of Allah

- Example: When witnessing beauty, nature, or reflecting on creation

Alḥamdulillāh

- Meaning: "All praise is due to Allah"

- Use: Gratitude for blessings, recovery, or even life's simple moments

- Example: After completing a task or when something good happens

Allāhu Akbar

- Meaning: "Allah is greater"

- Use: Recognizing God's greatness over everything—including ego, addiction, or struggle

- Example: In moments of difficulty, or to shift focus from worldly distractions

Lā ilāha illa Allāh

- Meaning: "There is no god but Allah"

- Use: The core declaration of faith and spiritual surrender

- Example: As a grounding affirmation when feeling lost or disconnected

Astaghfirullāh

- Meaning: "I seek forgiveness from Allah"

- Use: In repentance, self-inventory, or emotional slips

- Example: When reflecting on past mistakes or seeking a clean slate

Ya Allāh

- Meaning: "O Allah"

- Use: A heartfelt call to God—can express need, longing, or surrender

- Example: When words fail, but the heart still reaches out

Ṣalawāt (Sending Blessings Upon the Prophet)

- Meaning: *Allāhumma ṣalli ʿalā Muḥammad* , "O Allah, send blessings upon Muhammad"

- Use: Brings spiritual peace, builds love for the Prophet (SAW), and is highly recommended

- Example: In moments of stress, gratitude, or silence

How to Practice *Dhikr*

- You can repeat these phrases silently, aloud, on prayer beads (misbaha), or mentally throughout the day.

- You don't need to be in ritual purity (*wudu*) to do *dhikr*, though it's recommended.

- *Dhikr* is a state of heart more than a ritual. It's about presence, not performance.

- Even one sincere *Subḥānallāh* from the heart is valuable.

"Surely in the remembrance of Allah do hearts find rest."

Qur'an, 13:28

Beginner's Path: Start Here

For those new to *dhikr* or in early recovery, starting with the full practice might feel overwhelming. Begin with this simplified version (approximately 10-15 minutes) and expand as you grow comfortable.

1. Be in *Wudu* if possible (physical and spiritual cleanliness)

2. Three Times: *Shahada* (reaffirming your foundation)

3. Thirty-Three Times: *Astaghfirullah* (seeking forgiveness)

4. Thirty-Three Times: *Subhan'Allah* (glory be to Allah)

5. Thirty-Three Times: *Alhamdulillah* (all praise belongs to Allah)

6. Thirty-Four Times: *Allahu Akbar* (Allah is greater)

7. Five Minutes: Quiet Meditation (simply being present with Allah)

This simplified practice incorporates the core elements while being manageable for beginners. As you develop consistency, you can gradually incorporate more elements from the complete practice.

The Complete Practice

You don't have to over complicate it. The point isn't to perform; it's to connect. Here's a simple *dhikr* flow you can start with and build on:

- Be in *Wudu* (if possible) Begin clean. The physical purification helps set the tone for the spiritual one.

- Three Times: *Shahada*, (*Ashhadu an la ilaha illa Allah, wa ashhadu anna Muhammadan Rasul Allah*)Reaffirm your foundation: the Oneness of Allah and the Prophethood of Muhammad (SAW).

- One Hundred Times: *Astaghfirullah*(I seek forgiveness from Allah.)Clean the heart through sincere repentance.

- Three Times: *Surah Ikhlas*, Remind yourself of the pure Oneness of Allah.

- One Time: *Surah Al-Fatiha* (The Opening)A prayer for guidance, mercy, and straightness.

- One Hundred Times: *A'udhu Billah* (I seek refuge with Allah.) Protection from distractions, internal and external.

- One Hundred Times: *Bismillah* (In the Name of Allah.) Begin everything with His Name on your tongue.

- One Hundred Times: *La ilaha illa Allah* (There is no god but Allah.)Strip away everything false and return to truth.

- Three Hundred Times: Allah (with the tongue) Let it rise from your heart to your lips.

- Three Hundred Times: Allah (in stillness, from the heart) Silent remembrance. Feel the vibration inside you.

- One Hundred Times: *Salawat* on the Prophet (SAW), (*Allahumma salli 'ala Muhammad wa 'ala aali Muhammad...*) Send blessings on the one who showed us the way.

- One Time: *Surah Al-Fatiha* to close. Seal the session with the prayer of Opening.

- *Muraqabah* (Meditation) Sit quietly. Breathe. Let the Names settle inside you. No effort. Just being.

Notes on Practice:

- Sacred Times: Before *Fajr* (dawn) and just after *Maghrib* (sunset) are especially powerful—moments when the day itself is in transition, and the heart can shift too.

- Gentleness Over Force: If you can't complete the full routine, do what you can with presence. Quality always matters more than quantity.

- Consistency: Once every 24 hours. Make it as normal as brushing your teeth—something you do without needing to be convinced.

- Feel It: Let the words move through you. Don't just say them. Resonate with them.

- Time Required: The complete practice typically takes 30-45 minutes. The beginner's path takes 10-15 minutes. Either way, consider it sacred time that you're reclaiming from the chaos of everyday life.

Common Struggles with *Dhikr* (And How to Handle Them)

Nobody starts this path perfectly. That's not the point. Struggles are part of the process—and honestly, they're signs you're doing the work.

Here's a few common things that come up during dhikr practice, and some ways to handle them:

1. Mind Wandering

What happens: You're reciting, and the next thing you know, you're thinking about groceries, bills, that weird thing you said three years ago.

What to do:It's normal. When you notice the mind has drifted, just gently bring it back. Don't beat yourself up. Every time you pull it back, it's like lifting a weight—you're building strength.

2. Feeling Numb or Emotionless

What happens: You say the words, but you feel nothing. It's mechanical.

What to do: Keep going. The heart wakes up in layers. Some days, you'll feel a deep connection. Some days you'll feel flat. The practice works even when you don't feel it immediately. Think of it like watering a seed underground; you can't always see the growth yet.

3. Falling Asleep

What happens: You get still... and the next thing you know, you're out cold.

What to do: Adjust your position. Sit upright rather than lying down. *Dhikr* is not intended to make you fall asleep. It's meant to wake you up. If you're exhausted, maybe shorten the session that day, but try to keep the habit alive.

4. Doubting If It's "Working"

What happens: You wonder if you're wasting your time, if you're doing it wrong, if you're just saying words into the air.

What to do: This is the mind's trick. It wants immediate results like it's ordering food at a drive-thru. But *dhikr* is heart work, not head work. Trust the unseen. The roots are growing even when the surface looks quiet.

5. Getting Bored

What happens: You think, "This again? Same words, same routine."

What to do: Remember: the words remain the same, but you grow. Every recitation is a new opportunity to connect. You are not just repeating phrases; you are tuning your being back into resonance with Allah.

Connection to Recovery

Just as the 11th Step emphasizes "prayer and meditation to improve our conscious contact with God," *dhikr* serves as a daily spiritual practice that strengthens our connection to Allah. Like daily inventory in recovery, *dhikr* helps us clear away the mental and emotional debris that accumulates each day. It creates a sacred space where we can reconnect with our higher purpose and the source of our strength.

Final Tip:

Lower the bar, raise the floor.

Some days you'll hit it strong. Some days, you'll barely manage a few minutes. That's life. Just stay consistent. Even the smallest, sincere remembrance echoes far beyond what you can imagine.

> *"So remember Me; I will remember you. And be grateful to Me and do not deny Me."*
>
> Qur'an, 2:152

That's all the proof you need to keep showing up.

The goal of *dhikr* is about opening your heart. It's about tuning back into the Divine Presence that's already closer to you than your own soul. Every moment you spend in remembrance, whether it feels powerful or painfully dry, is a step back toward your true home, your *fitrah*. Keep going. Keep showing up. Resonance will come. Connection will come. Allah never wastes the effort of those who seek Him.

Wudu

A Brief Guide to *Wudu* (Ablution)

For non-Muslim readers who may be unfamiliar with this practice. I am including the following explanation and guide.

In Islam, *wudu* (pronounced woo-doo) is a ritual washing performed before prayer. It serves as both a physical and spiritual purification, preparing the worshiper to stand before God in a state of cleanliness and mindfulness. The Qur'an and the teachings of the Prophet Muhammad (SAW) establish the practice's deep roots.

> *"When a Muslim—or a believer—washes his face, every sin he contemplated with his eyes will be washed away with the water... When he washes his hands, every sin they committed will be washed away... When he washes his feet, every sin his feet walked toward will be washed away... until he emerges purified from sins."*
>
> Prophet Muhammad (SAW), Sahih Muslim 244

Wudu involves washing specific parts of the body in a set order: the hands, mouth, nose, face, arms, head, ears, and feet. It typically takes just a few minutes and is done with plain water. Muslims perform *wudu* several times a day, most commonly before each of the five daily prayers. It is also required after certain actions, such as using the restroom, falling asleep, or anything that invalidates a state of minor purity. Many Muslims also perform *wudu* before reading the Qur'an, before leaving home, or when seeking spiritual clarity, treating it as a physical and spiritual preparation for sacred acts.

Wudu is more than hygiene. It is an act of intention and humility. It creates a pause in the day, clears distractions, and refocuses the heart. Many Muslims also find it grounding during moments of emotional or spiritual stress.

Though simple in form, *wudu* symbolizes a larger truth: that spiritual readiness begins with purification, and that connection to the Divine requires both outward cleanliness and inward awareness.

This guide outlines the Sunnah (Prophetic) method of performing *wudu*, based on authentic hadith.

Steps of Sunnah Wudu:

1. Intention (*Niyyah*) — Begin with the internal intention to purify yourself for the sake of Allah. No words need to be spoken aloud.

2. Say "*Bismillah*" — Begin by saying: *Bismillah* ("In the Name of Allah").

3. Wash the Hands (3 times) — Wash both hands up to the wrists, starting with the right.

4. Rinse the Mouth (3 times) — Swish water around the mouth and expel it.

5. Rinse the Nose (3 times) — Gently inhale water into the nostrils and blow it out.

6. Wash the Face (3 times) — From the hairline to the chin and from ear to ear.

7. Wash the Arms (3 times) — Wash the right arm, then the left, from fingertips to elbows.

8. Wipe the Head (Once) — With wet hands, wipe over the head from front to back and back to front.

9. Wipe the Ears (Once) — Use the index fingers to wipe the inside and the thumbs for the outer parts of the ears.

10. Wash the Feet (3 times) — Wash the right foot, then the left, including the ankles.

Recommended Du'a After Wudu:

"Ashhadu an la ilaha illa Allah, wahdahu la sharika lah, wa ashhadu anna Muhammadan 'abduhu wa rasuluh." "I bear witness that there is no god but Allah alone, with no partner, and I bear witness that Muhammad is His servant and Messenger."

"Allahumma aj'alni min at-tawwabeen, waj'alni min al-mutatahhireen." "O Allah, make me among those who repent often and those who purify themselves."

Glossary - Islamic Terms

Adab—In Islamic spirituality, *adab* refers to proper manners, conduct, and spiritual etiquette—how one carries themselves in the presence of Allah, others, and the self. It includes humility, sincerity, and the alignment of outward behavior with inward reverence.

Allah—The Arabic name for God, used by Muslims to refer to the One and Only Creator, Sustainer, and Judge. Unlike the English word "God," Allah is linguistically singular, without plural or gender, and is universally used by Arabic-speaking Jews and Christians as well.

Deen—An Arabic term often translated as "religion," but its meaning is far more encompassing. *Deen* refers to a complete way of life rooted in submission to Allah. It includes belief, worship, ethics, behavior, and law. In Islam, *deen* is not limited to rituals or personal spirituality—it shapes how one interacts with others, navigates hardship, and pursues justice. The Qur'an describes Islam as *"deen al-ḥaqq"* (the true way of life) because it aligns the human soul with divine order. For those in recovery, embracing *deen* means allowing spiritual principles to guide not just private belief, but daily action, service, and transformation.

Dhikr—Meaning "remembrance," dhikr is the act of remembering Allah, often through repeated invocation of divine names or phrases such as *SubhanAllah* (Glory be to God), *Alhamdulillah* (All praise is due to God), and *La ilaha illa Allah* (There is no god but God). In Sufi and recovery contexts, *dhikr* is a form of spiritual grounding and awakening.

Fitrah—The natural, pure disposition upon which every human being is born—an innate recognition of truth, morality, and the Creator. In Islamic theology, fitrah is not erased by sin but can be covered or corrupted. Recovery is seen here as a return to fitrah, not reinvention of the self.

Hadith—A hadith is a reported saying, action, or silent approval of the Prophet Muhammad (SAW). Alongside the Qur'an, hadiths are primary sources of Islamic knowledge and law. They are classified by authenticity and often serve as spiritual or ethical guidance.

Iman—Often translated as "faith" or "belief," *iman* refers to inner conviction and trust in Allah. It is deeper than intellectual assent—it encompasses belief in the unseen, acceptance of divine guidance, and reliance on God's mercy. Classical scholars describe iman as something that increases with obedience and decreases with sin.

Islam—Literally meaning "surrender" or "submission," Islam is the path of submitting one's will to Allah. It is both the name of the religion and the spiritual act of turning oneself over to Divine guidance. The root of the word shares ties with *salaam* (peace) and *taslīm* (submission).

Muraqabah—Spiritual watchfulness—being inwardly alert and conscious of Allah's presence at all times. It's often described as the practice of observing the heart with awareness, akin to being in a constant state of *ihsan* (spiritual excellence).

Muslim—A person who submits to the will of Allah. To be Muslim is not merely to identify with a religion, but to surrender one's ego, desires, and decisions to the Creator. The word is derived from the same root as Islam and implies active submission, not passive belief.

Nafs—The self or ego—often understood as the locus of desire, identity, and lower impulses. In the Islamic tradition, the *nafs* exists on a spectrum, from the base commanding self (*nafs al-ammārah*) to the soul at peace (*nafs al-muṭma'innah*).

Nafs al-Ammāra—"The Commanding Self"—the lowest and most dangerous form of the ego. This is the part of the self that issues demands based on desire and pride, without regard for ethics or consequence. The Qur'an names it as a source of evil unless restrained by Divine mercy.

Niyyah—Intention. Every action in Islam is judged according to its *niyyah*, and even mundane acts can become worship if the intention is sincere. In recovery, niyyah aligns with clarity of purpose—it's not just what you do, but why you do it.

Qabd—Spiritual contraction. *Qabd* refers to a state in which the heart feels constricted, dry, or distant from Divine presence. It is the opposite of *bast* (expansion) and is considered a normal part of the spiritual path. Rather than a sign of failure, *qabd* may be a test of sincerity or a divine invitation to deeper reliance and trust.

Qadr—Divine decree or destiny. *Qadr* refers to the belief that everything that happens—past, present, and future—occurs by the will and knowledge of Allah. It does not negate human choice, but places that choice within the boundaries of Allah's all-encompassing wisdom.

Qurb—Closeness or nearness to Allah—not spatial, but spiritual. To have *qurb* is to feel connected to the Divine, to experience intimacy with the Creator through worship, remembrance, and sincerity. In Sufi literature, *qurb* is the fruit of spiritual striving.

Rida—Contentment with Allah's decree. While *sabr* is bearing hardship with patience, *rida* is embracing it with peace. Scholars describe *rida* as the hallmark of a mature soul—one that no longer argues with the events of life but accepts them as Divine wisdom in action.

Rizq—Provision, whatever Allah allots to a person in this life, from material wealth to time, knowledge, healing, and even clarity. *Rizq* is not earned by merit, but granted by Divine will, though seeking it through lawful means is encouraged.

Sabr—Patience, perseverance, and endurance. It is more than just waiting—it is remaining firm in obedience and trust even when hardship strikes. The Qur'an repeatedly connects *sabr* with success and Divine reward.

Salaam—An Arabic word meaning "peace." It is used as both a greeting—*As-salaamu 'alaykum* ("Peace be upon you")—and a concept that reflects the inner and outer tranquility promoted in Islam.

SAW—(*Ṣallā Allāhu 'alayhi wa sallam*) Abbreviation of the Arabic phrase, meaning "May Allah send blessings and peace upon him," used after mentioning the Prophet Muhammad. This replaces the Arabic ligature for compatibility with print formats.

Shahada—The Islamic testimony of faith: *Ashhadu an lā ilāha illa Allah, wa ashhadu anna Muḥammadan rasūl Allah* — "I bear witness that there is no god but Allah, and Muhammad is the Messenger of Allah." It marks the entry into Islam and is the most fundamental declaration of belief.

Shari'ah—The sacred law derived from the Qur'an and the Sunnah. It governs all aspects of a Muslim's life, from ritual practice to ethics. While often misunderstood as merely legalistic, *shari'ah* is ultimately a roadmap to Divine proximity and justice.□ Mentioned briefly in the introduction as the grounding structure that complements spiritual transformation.

Shaytan—The devil in Islamic tradition, understood as a conscious, external force that invites people toward self-destruction, disconnection from God, and indulgence in the lower desires. *Shaytan* fuels negative thinking, tempts the ego, and thrives on distraction, isolation, and false promises offered by the *dunya* (worldly life).

Sheikh—An Arabic title meaning "elder" or "leader." In Islamic contexts, it can refer to a tribal leader, a learned scholar, or a spiritual guide. In Sufi or spiritual traditions, a sheikh is often someone who offers mentorship and guidance on the path to Allah, based on wisdom, experience, and adherence to the Qur'an and Sunnah. The term is used with respect but does not always imply formal authority.

Shirk—The gravest sin in Islam: associating partners with Allah or giving divine attributes to anything other than the Creator. It includes idol worship, but also more subtle forms, such as placing ultimate trust or devotion in one's ego, desires, or other people.

Suhba—Spiritual companionship. In the Islamic tradition—especially among Sufi circles—*suhba* is the transformative fellowship of being in the company of sincere, God-conscious people. The Prophet (SAW) emphasized the power of being with righteous companions.

Sufi—A term used to describe one who follows the inward, spiritual path of Islam—seeking proximity to Allah through purification of the heart, remembrance, and surrender. While not a separate sect, Sufism refers to the mystical tradition embedded within Islamic orthodoxy.

Sunnah—The way and teachings of the Prophet Muhammad (SAW), including his actions, sayings, and approvals. The Sunnah provides practical guidance on how to live in alignment with the Qur'an and is a primary source of Islamic law and spirituality. In recovery terms, the Sunnah can be seen as the model behavior of someone who is spiritually awake and living in service, humility, and integrity.

Taqwa—God-consciousness, often translated as "piety" or "reverent fear." *Taqwa* is a protective shield against sin, rooted in awareness of Allah's presence and accountability to Him. The Qur'an says the most honored in the sight of Allah are those with the most *taqwa*.

Tariqa—A spiritual path or order within Sufism. Each tariqa has its own lineage and methods for purifying the soul and drawing closer to Allah, often under the guidance of a *sheikh*. The word literally means "path" or "way."

Taslim—Surrender. Closely related to Islam, *taslim* means the inner act of handing over one's will to Allah—not in defeat, but in sacred trust. It's the posture of the heart that says, "I accept, I trust, I submit."

Tawakkul—Reliance upon Allah. *Tawakkul* is not passive resignation—it is active trust. The believer takes all necessary action, but leaves the outcome to Allah with full faith that He is sufficient.

Ummah—The global community of Muslims, united by faith in Allah and following the teachings of the Prophet Muhammad (SAW). The concept transcends race, nationality, and language, emphasizing spiritual brotherhood and collective responsibility.

Waswas—Whispers or intrusive thoughts from *Shaytan* or the *nafs* that sow doubt, confusion, or temptation. These thoughts are often subtle and persistent, aimed at disrupting spiritual focus or pulling the believer away from remembrance.

Wudu—Ritual ablution. *Wudu* is the physical purification Muslims perform before prayer, involving the washing of hands, face, arms, head, and feet. It prepares the body and mind for sacred connection, turning even routine washing into a spiritual act of intention and presence. Many find *wudu* grounding and clarifying, especially in moments of anxiety or relapse temptation.

Glossary - Recovery Terms

Admission—The spiritual act of telling the truth—often for the first time. In Step One, admission means acknowledging powerlessness over addiction and admitting that life has become unmanageable. This is the crack where healing begins.

Big Book—The foundational text of Alcoholics Anonymous, officially titled Alcoholics Anonymous. It contains personal stories, the 12 Steps, spiritual principles, and guidance for working the program. Often quoted with reverence in recovery spaces.

Character Defects—Shortcomings or harmful tendencies—such as pride, fear, selfishness, and dishonesty—that keep a person spiritually blocked. Steps Six and Seven deal with becoming willing to let these be removed and asking God to do so. These can be interpreted as veils over the heart.

Collapse—A metaphor used when describing rock bottom, the breaking point where self-will fails. This emotional or spiritual breakdown is often a necessary prelude to surrender and transformation.

Craving (Phenomenon of Craving)—A mental and physical compulsion to use substances despite consequences. In the Big Book, it's referred to as a phenomenon that never occurs in the average temperate drinker. It's used to describe a form of spiritual slavery—where the soul is hijacked by appetite.

Dry Drunk—Someone who is abstinent but has not achieved emotional or spiritual recovery. The behavior remains driven by ego, resentment, or control. Abstinence alone is not the goal—transformation is.

Ego—The false self that clings to control, pride, and fear. In recovery, ego is often the underlying disease beneath addiction. Simply aligned with the *nafs*, especially nafs al-ammāra, the commanding self. (*Also the acronym EGO = Easing God Out*)

Euphoric Recall—A distorted memory in which one remembers the highs of substance use and forgets the consequences. Euphoric recall glamorizes destruction and feeds relapse. Common in recovery, it's the whisper of the lower self trying to pull the seeker back into illusion.

F.E.A.R.—A commonly reinterpreted acronym for fear in recovery circles. It has multiple meanings

False Evidence Appearing Real

Fear Everything And Run

Face Everything And Recover

Each version reframes fear as a crossroads moment—either relapse or renewal.

F.I.N.E.—An acronym used sarcastically when someone insists they're "fine," but it's clear they are not. It stands for:

Fed up, Insecure, Neurotic, and Emotional

Finally I Need Everyone

It humorously reveals the danger of hiding pain behind forced composure.

Fellowship—The spiritual and communal lifeblood of recovery. Fellowship is more than meetings—it's the lived connection between seekers on the same path. Synonymous with suhba, the Islamic concept of spiritual companionship.

Geographic Cure (or Pulling a Geographic)—The attempt to solve one's addiction or emotional issues by moving to a new place. "If I change the scenery, I'll change inside." In reality, the addict brings themselves wherever they go. It reflects the illusion that the external will fix the internal.

Higher Power—AA's flexible term for any power greater than oneself. It leaves space for the individual to define spirituality on their own terms. This work honors this openness while reorienting the seeker toward the Islamic understanding of God (Allah).

Insanity—As described in Step Two: doing the same thing over and over again and expecting different results. It includes the madness of returning to addiction despite consequences and the delusion that one can control the outcome.

Inventory—A personal moral inventory—a fearless and searching examination of one's fears, resentments, harms, and patterns. Introduced in Step Four and continued as a practice of accountability. Well covered parallel with *muhasaba* (spiritual self-review).

Keep Coming Back—A phrase said in AA meetings to encourage those who relapse, struggle, or feel unworthy. It conveys unconditional love and the belief that healing is always possible. In tone, it echoes Allah's mercy.

Old Timer—A respected member of the recovery community who has maintained long-term sobriety, often for decades. Old timers are valued for their lived experience, depth of insight, and steady presence in the fellowship.

One Day at a Time—The cornerstone mindset of recovery. Instead of worrying about forever, the addict is asked to focus only on today. It fosters presence and reduces anxiety. This is aligned with tawakkul—trust in Allah's daily provision.

Pink Cloud—A phase in early sobriety marked by euphoria and idealism. Everything feels amazing—until emotional or spiritual work hits. Often followed by disillusionment or a crash. While it's not directly addressed in the work it bears mentioning because it resonates with the highs and lows of awakening.

Powerlessness—The condition of having lost control over substance use. Step One begins with this acknowledgment—not as defeat, but as the first moment of truth. Moment of clarity treats it as sacred honesty.

Resentment—Lingering anger or blame—described in AA as "the number one offender." Resentment blocks spiritual growth and fuels relapse. Mentioned many times through the work.

Rigorous Honesty—Telling the full truth about oneself, even when it's painful. Recovery cannot happen without it. The work treats it as both a moral and spiritual imperative, echoing the Islamic virtue of sidq (truthfulness).

Rock Bottom—The lowest point of one's descent—emotional, physical, or spiritual. It often marks the beginning of surrender. Think of it is the fertile soil where ego dies and truth can take root.

Self-Will—The obsessive drive to control life through one's own plans and desires. It is the fuel of addiction and the antithesis of surrender. There is a direct link with self-will with the diseases of the heart and the domination of the ego.

Service—Helping others as a way to stay sober and spiritually grounded. Service is Step Twelve in action. It's described as the fruit of true awakening—where love is put into motion.

Spiritual Awakening—The result of working all twelve steps. It may come as a sudden clarity or a slow unfolding, but always involves a shift from self-centeredness to surrender. We treat it as a Divine gift rather than an earned outcome.

Spiritual Bypass—Using spiritual ideas to avoid real emotional work. For example, saying "It's God's will" to avoid making amends. Mentioned as a critique of false piety—real faith requires honesty and action.

Sponsor—A sober mentor who guides others through the Steps. Not a therapist or guru, but a trusted fellow traveler. The sponsor is seen as a contemporary form of the spiritual elder or guide.

Stinking Thinking—A recovery term for the distorted thought patterns that often precede relapse. It includes rationalization, self-pity, resentment, catastrophizing, and the illusion of control. Even when sober, an addict may still suffer from stinking thinking if the underlying spiritual disease remains untreated.

Terminal Uniqueness—The belief that one is "different" and therefore not subject to the same rules. It isolates the addict and blocks healing. In spiritual language, it is the ego posing as individuality.

The Promises—A set of hopeful outcomes described in the Big Book, traditionally read after Step Nine. These promises include freedom from fear, peace of mind, and a new sense of purpose. They are seen not as guarantees, but as the natural results of spiritual growth and consistent action in the program.

The Rooms—A colloquial term for AA meetings and the spaces of fellowship and transformation. To be "in the rooms" means to be actively engaged in the recovery path. The fellowship treats these rooms as sacred gathering spaces.

Triggers—People, places, emotions, or memories that increase the urge to use. Recovery requires identifying and neutralizing these triggers. Spiritually, they are treated as moments of Divine test and response.

Working the Steps—Going through all Twelve Steps—not just attending meetings or reading the literature. It is the heart of AA's process. Generally recovery is entirely structured around this commitment to action and surrender.

Works Cited

Partial List of Works Cited

Primary Islamic Texts

- The Qur'an, Sahih International Translation. Abul-Qasim Publishing House, 1997.

- Sahih al-Bukhari, trans. Dr. Muhammad Muhsin Khan. Dar-us-Salam Publications.

- Sahih Muslim, trans. Nasiruddin al-Khattab. Dar-us-Salam Publications.

- Sunan al-Tirmidhi, trans. Abu Khaliyl. Dar-us-Salam Publications.

- Sunan Ibn Majah, trans. Nasiruddin al-Khattab. Dar-us-Salam Publications.

- Sunan Abi Dawud, trans. Nasiruddin al-Khattab. Dar-us-Salam Publications.

- Musnad Ahmad ibn Hanbal, multiple volumes, Dar al-Fikr.

- Shu'ab al-Iman by Imam al-Bayhaqi. Dar al-Kutub al-'Ilmiyyah.

Classical & Sufi Works

- Al-Ghazali, Abu Hamid. Ihya' 'Ulum al-Din (The Revival of the Religious Sciences). Trans. various editions.

- Al-Ghazali. The Alchemy of Happiness. Trans. Claud Field. Islamic Book Trust, 2007.

- Ibn Ata'illah al-Iskandari. Al-Hikam al-'Ata'iyyah (The Book of Wisdoms). Various editions and commentaries.

- Ibn Qayyim al-Jawziyya. Madarij al-Salikin (Stations of the Wayfarers). Trans. various.

- Imam al-Haddad. The Book of Assistance. Trans. Mostafa al-Badawi. Fons Vitae, 2003.

- Shaykh Abdul Qadir al-Jilani. Futuh al-Ghayb (Revelations of the Unseen). Various editions.

- Sahl al-Tustari. Tustari Tafsir / Sayings of the Sufi Masters. Various translations.

- Rabia al-Adawiyya. Prayers of Rabia (Traditional attributions, recorded in classical Sufi literature).

- Rumi, Jalal ad-Din. The Essential Rumi. Trans. Coleman Barks. HarperOne, 1995.

- Rumi. Fihi Ma Fihi (It Is What It Is). Trans. A.J. Arberry or Coleman Barks.

- Attar of Nishapur. The Conference of the Birds. Trans. Afkham Darbandi and Dick Davis. Penguin Classics, 1984.

Alcoholics Anonymous / Recovery Texts

- Alcoholics Anonymous: The Story of How Many Thousands of Men and Women Have Recovered from Alcoholism ("The Big Book"). 4th ed., Alcoholics Anonymous World Services, Inc., 2001.

- Twelve Steps and Twelve Traditions. Alcoholics Anonymous World Services,

Inc., 1981.

- Living Sober. Alcoholics Anonymous World Services, Inc., 1975.

Additional References

- Al-Nawawi. Forty Hadith of Imam Nawawi. Trans. Ezzeddin Ibrahim and Denys Johnson-Davies.

- Tabarani, Al-Hafidh. Mu'jam al-Awsat. Dar al-Kutub al-Ilmiyyah.

About the author

James H. is a recovering alcoholic and American revert to Islam. His work explores the intersection of Islamic spirituality and addiction recovery, with a focus on practical application and personal transformation.

He is the host of the *Path of the Sober Seeker* podcast and the founder of the Pathways Collective, a platform dedicated to spiritual growth, recovery, and honest reflection.

To learn more, visit **soberseekerpath.com**